Politics of the Very Worst

SEMIOTEXT(E) FOREIGN AGENTS SERIES

Jim Fleming & Sylvère Lotringer, Editors

INSIDE & OUT OF BYZANTIUM
Nina Zivancevic

COMMUNISTS LIKE US
Félix Guattari & Toni Negri

ECSTASY OF COMMUNICATION
Jean Baudrillard

SIMULATIONS
Jean Baudrillard

GERMANIA
Heiner Müller

POPULAR DEFENSE & ECOLOGICAL STRUGGLES
Paul Virilio

IN THE SHADOW OF THE SILENT MAJORITIES
Jean Baudrillard

FORGET FOUCAULT
Jean Baudrillard

ASSASSINATION RHAPSODY
Derek Pell

REMARKS ON MARX
Michel Foucault

STILL BLACK, STILL STRONG
Dhoruba Bin Wahad, Mumia Abu-Jamal & Assata Shakur

SADNESS AT LEAVING
Erje Ayden

POLITICS OF THE VERY WORST
Paul Virilio

LOOKING BACK ON THE END OF THE WORLD
Jean Baudrillard, Paul Virilio, et al.

NOMADOLOGY: THE WAR MACHINE
Gilles Deleuze & Félix Guattari

PURE WAR
Paul Virilio & Sylvère Lotringer

METATRON
Sol Yurick

BOLO'BOLO
P.M.

ON THE LINE
Gilles Deleuze & Félix Guattari

SPEED AND POLITICS
Paul Virilio

DRIFTWORKS
Jean-François Lyotard

69 WAYS TO PLAY THE BLUES
Jürg Laederach

THE POLITICS OF TRUTH
Michel Foucault

CHAOSOPHY
Félix Guattari

SOFT SUBVERSIONS
Félix Guattari

Politics of the Very Worst

Paul Virilio

An Interview by Philippe Petit

Translated by Michael Cavaliere
Edited by Sylvère Lotringer

Semiotext(e)

Special thanks to Brian Wong and Jeffrey Rueppel
for their work on notes and the index.

Translated from the original French edition
published by Les éditions Textuel, Paris, 1996.

Semiotext(e)
501 Philosophy Hall
Columbia University
New York, New York 10027
Phone: 212-854-3956

Autonomedia Distribution
55 South Eleventh Street
POB 568 Williamsburgh Station
Brooklyn, New York 11211
Phone & Fax: 718-963-2603

Printed in the United States of America

CONTENTS

Paul Virilio: A Profile

Paul Virilio was born in France in 1932 to an Italian Communist father, who was an illegal alien in France, and a Breton Catholic mother. They spent the war in the devastated North Atlantic region. *War baby,* as Virilio likes to say. He was fifteen years old when Allied bombs fell on Nantes, where his family had sought refuge. For this urban planner, the destruction of the urban setting had been his testing ground, the fragility of the city his first concern.

After France was liberated from German occupation, Virilio attended the École des Métiers d'Art in Paris, with the idea of becoming a master glass artist. He worked with Braque in Varengeville and with Matisse at Saint-Paul-de-Vence. He took classes at the Sorbonne with Vladimir Jankelevitch, Jean Wahl and Raymond Aron,[1] mastered philosophy, and developed a passion for architecture and Gestalt psychology.

At 18, he became a Christian. He closely associated himself with Father Pierre and the priest-worker movement.[2] His present preoccupation with the homeless goes back to his involvement with the *Sans-Logis* in the winter of 1954. In the summer of 1958, on a beach in Normandy, he had a revelation of the German "bunkers" and decided to study the architecture of war (*Bunker Archeology*).[3] Unlike many of his colleagues at the time, he actively took part in the events of May 1968. He occupied the Odeon theater in Paris and dreamed of a city that would be a stage. Ten years later, he joined Alain Joxe's Sociology of Defense Group[4] at the École des Hautes Études en Sciences Sociales. With his friend Georges Perec,[5] he created the "Critical Space" series at Éditions Galilée in Paris. He also actively contributed to major magazines *Esprit, Causes Communes,* and *Traverses*.[6]

With Félix Guattari,[7] he started the *Radio Tomate* free radio in 1979, and created a social service for the homeless. An architect associated with the "Brutalist" school, he stopped practicing architecture after 1968 and has been writing on the current technological revolution ever since. He is now recognized as the philosopher of speed and an authority on war technology. In 1975, he became director of the Special School of Architecture in Paris. He recently retired to write his book on the Accident, to be published in the year 2000.

From transportation revolution to communications revolution

From
transportation
revolution
to
communications
revolution

“Will we be able to achieve a democracy in real-time, in *live time*, immediate and ubiquitous?”

I

From Transportation Revolution To Communications Revolution

You are an observatory of technological revolutions all by yourself. Since *Bunker Archaeology*, your first book, which was published in France in 1975, you have not stopped denouncing the perils of technology and the devastation of progress in both the military and civil domains. Aren't you afraid of being perceived as a somewhat old-fashioned cultural critic? After all, technological progress does not have only negative effects.

As Beaumarchais said, "There is no flattering praise without the freedom to blame." Yet without the freedom to criticize technology, there is no "technical progress" either, only a conditioning.... And when this conditioning becomes cybernetic, as is happening today with the new technologies, the threat becomes considerable.

We are no longer in the nineteenth century but at the end of the twentieth century, and today the debate about the new technologies seems to block out what we lived throughout the twentieth century in terms of progress. In the nineteenth century, people could be naive with respect to technical progress and even to social progress. We could even excuse them for not envisioning the totalitarian dimension of the new technologies : the railroad, and the radio, the negative use and pollution, whether psychological, geological or atmospheric, of the new technologies. I think that today, at the dawn of the twenty-first century, we have to acknowledge the negativity of a progress that remains progress, but that is no longer an omnipotent progress, one idealized by a philosophy that has no distance in relation to the hidden side of positivism.

The new technologies are cybernetic technologies. The new information technologies organize networks of relations and information, and, as such, they quite obviously convey the perspective of a humanity that is not only unified but also reduced to uniformity. I believe that the question of the accident, the question of pollution, and the question of the ravages of progress, constantly repeated throughout the twentieth century, are once again on the agenda. Praising the merits of the new technologies is certainly useful for the advertisement of new products, but I don't think that this is useful for the politics of the new technologies. From now on, it is necessary to determine what is negative in what seems positive. We know that we can only advance in technology by recognizing its specific accident, its specific negativity...

Today, the new technologies convey a certain type of accident, one that is no longer local and precisely situated, like the sinking of the *Titanic* or the derailment of a train, but *general*, an accident that immediately affects the entire world. This is quite obvious when we are told that the Internet has a worldwide vocation. Yet the accident of the Internet, or that of other technologies of the same nature, also represents the emergence of a total — not to say integral — accident. And that situation has no reference. We don't know yet, perhaps with the exception of the stock market crash, what an integral accident could be, an accident that would involve everyone at the same time.

The production of real time by the new technologies, like it or not, is the implementation of a time that has no relationship to historical time. Real time is world time. All of History happened in local time, for example the local time of France, America, Italy, Paris, or wherever. And the potential for instantaneous interaction and interactivity creates the possibility of achieving a single time, a time that only refers to the universal time of astronomy. This is an unprecedented event. It is a positive event, and yet at the same time an event full of negative possibilities, and I say this because I am a child of the twentieth century, and not the twenty-first.

So I am not a prophet of doom, but simply a true lover of the new technologies...

By the way, let me remind you that ten years ago, I was unanimously awarded the national Grand Prize for criticism by the jury of the Department of Planning, Housing and Transportation!

In your work, there is a continuity between your analyses concerning the transportation revolution of the nineteenth century and the virtual technologies of our own *fin de siècle*. The analogy that you make between the two is based on the notion of speed. Why do you attach so much importance to that notion?

The question of speed is central. It pertains to the question of economy. Not only is speed a threat, insofar as it is capitalized and tyrannical, but it is also life itself. Speed and wealth go hand in hand. To give a philosophical definition of speed, we can say that it is not a phenomenon, but rather the relationship between phenomena. In other words, it is relativity itself. We can go even further and say that speed is a milieu. It doesn't just involve the time between two points, but a milieu that is provoked by a vehicle. This vehicle can be either metabolic: consider the role of chivalry in history; or technical: the role of the ship in maritime conquest, railroads or transatlantic planes — and it governs societies. The horse influenced history with the great conquerors, while the navy influenced colonization. As Michelet wrote, "He who says great colony says great navy." The navy is a type of speed. Thus, for me, speed is my milieu.

Why?

Because I am a *Blitzkrieg* baby. I was born in 1932 and ever since my early childhood, I found myself confronted with the speed of war and the speed of communication thanks to the radio — including Radio Free France.[8]

What connection do you see between speed and power?

Power and speed are inseparable just as wealth and speed are inseparable. Power means, above all, dromocratic power — *dromos* comes from the Greek and means "race"— and every society is a "race society." Whether in ancient societies through the role of chivalry (the first Roman bankers were horsemen) or in maritime power through the conquest of the seas, power is always the power to control a territory with messengers, modes of transportation and communication. Independent of the economy of wealth, an approach to politics is impossible without an approach to the economy of speed. The role of speed differs according to the society in question. The Middle Ages had traveling pigeons with Jacques Coeur, the great financier of the time. Colonial society had the maritime power of England and France. Post–WWII society had air power with supersonic planes capable of breaking the sound barrier in the fifties. Global society is currently in a gestation period and cannot be understood without the speed of light or the automatic quotations of the stock markets in Wall Street, Tokyo, or London.

Power is essentially that which stimulates movement...

Speed is power itself. The figure of the pharaoh, a classical image though surprisingly forgotten, is an eloquent one. Everyone has a mental image of King Tutankhamen with both hands crossed on his chest. This image can be seen in the tomb. In one hand, he holds a whip and in the other a hook. Some archaeologists have asserted that the whip is a fly-swatter — a fly-swatter as a sign of pharaonic power is just nonsense. The whip was actually used to accelerate the chariot of war, while the hook was used to slow it down, to pull back the reins. Therefore, pharaonic power, like all power, is at once restraint, brake, wisdom and acceleration. This is true of the great pontiff, the great *Conducator* Ceausescu and the great helmsman. The image of Mao Tse–tung, Ceausescu or the pharaoh is always the same. All of them lead the society that they rule, direct its energies and determine its rhythm.

You said, "Power is always the power to grab." Isn't it possible to imagine a power whose function would be to facilitate the emancipation of the citizens. Aren't you disappointed by the ideal of the Enlightenment?

I am, of course, a democrat. I always have been, yet in my opinion there is no power without laws or regulations. Regulation of a book, of a constitution, and thus of a justice. There is a justice of wealth and economy, thus one of distribution. There is also an economy and a justice of speed. In the past, the nobility was originally a class of speed just like the cavalry. All the hick had was his cows! The question of speed is actually that of democratization. Ancient societies only implemented relative speeds : those of the horse or ship, or rather the speed of certain vehicles such as the train or car. Now, these speeds being relative, they could still be democratized. It is not by chance that the first ancient democracy, the Greek democracy, is a democracy of the *triere*, the fastest ship of its time. As stated in the Constitution of Athenians: "Those who govern the ship govern the City." Since speed was relative in the first democratic society, many men were needed to maneuver the triere, or to row. The need for manpower allowed for a fair distribution. This has been true of all relative speeds up to the plane. However, as soon as the era changed and the absolute speed of electromagnetic waves was reached, or real time, the question of the democratization of absolute speed came up.

You mean of absolute movement...

Yes, because the nature of absolute speed is also to be absolute power, absolute and instantaneous control, in other words an almost divine power. Today, we have achieved the three attributes of the divine: ubiquity, instantaneity, immediacy; omnivoyance and omnipotence. This is no longer a question of democracy — this is tyranny.

"Will we be able to achieve a democracy of real time, *live* time, a democracy of immediacy and ubiquity?"

Multimedia confronts us with a question : will we be able to achieve a democracy of real time, *live* time, a democracy of immediacy and ubiquity? I don't think so, and those who are quick to say yes cannot be very serious.

Did the Industrial Revolution of the nineteenth century prefigure today's technological space–time?

It goes without saying that the Industrial Revolution inaugurated the transportation revolution. It is also curious to note how much the Industrial Revolution dominates the very term transportation revolution, whereas in my opinion the latter is more important by virtue of its sociopolitical, geopolitical and geostrategic consequences. Yet, the two revolutions were contemporary and influenced one another. The transportation revolution has considerably modified the milieu of our societies. The revolution of the railroads and the steam engine, which gave rise to the great ships and maritime power, has achieved a revolution of space–time. From the moment that society moves toward the attainment of an industrial speed, we move imperceptibly from geopolitics to chronopolitics.

When the railroads were launched in the nineteenth century, Audibert, the railroad engineer, said : "If we succeed in having trains arrive within the second, we will have provided humanity with the most effective instrument for the construction of the new world." This method is called chronopolitics. It is not yet cybernetics, but already chronopolitics. After that, there is a disaffection of the soil (which is not to say of the territory), which in turn causes the beginning of the end of peasantry and the city/country opposition in favor of the city, resulting in the large movement of rural populations toward industrial cities. Consequently, there is a considerable mutation in the populating site. Men will pile up in the cities around large businesses and the peasantry will become the proletariat.

The rapprochment of people, a Saint–Simonian myth that accompanied the transportation revolution, reappears today with authors who see computer science as a way of developing exchange and communication between citizens. I am thinking, for example, of *La Planète relationnelle* (*The Relational Planet*) by Albert Bressand and Catherine Distler, published in 1995 by Editions Flammarion. How do you explain the persistence of this communicational myth?

In the nineteenth century, it was thought that the railroad would create a world democracy and reunite the peoples of Europe into one single agora. The idea was that the railroads would favor conviviality and solidarity. Let me remind you that there were seaside trains or express trains that were very expensive and didn't go very far, from Paris to Deauville, for example; thus, there would be first, second and third classes. There, we have real "speed classes." You have to be rich to take the express, whereas the slow train is reserved for the poorest people who go to take a dip in the English Channel. A democratization of the railroads was thus already being organized around seaside leisure activities, and these railroads were no longer simply a means of channeling peasants toward the city, but also a way of discovering the sea, foreign countries — a lot of British went to Houlgate or other ports in France. We are thus faced with a playful dimension of the democratization of transportation.

So, does the idea that cyberspace can serve democracy seem absurd to you?

Very much so! Because every time there is progress in speed, we are told: democracy will follow; yet we know very well that this is not the case. To return to the example of the revolution of the railroads, remember that the Germans used the railroads to attack France in 1914. There is the illusion of a redemptory speed, the illusion that bringing populations together in the most extreme way will not bring about conflicts but love, that one must love one's distant neighbor as oneself. I believe that this is a major illusion today. In the nineteenth century, this misconception was understandable. At that time, progress was still a myth because the harm that it brings about could not be determined. It was normal then to believe in the completely beneficial nature of science and technology; this would be inconceivable in the 21st century. The 20th century has witnessed the havoc of progress, which doesn't mean that we must backtrack and deny the achievements of the Industrial Revolution and the Transportation Revolution. Today, there is an illusionism related to advertising. The Industrial Revolution would have been impossible without the invention of advertisement. Besides, our current school of thought was established thirty years ago by many Saint–Simonians,[9] and in particular by Emile de Girardin, the leader of the modern press who introduced advertisement in the press in order to free it from State control. Industry then saw the development of the advertisement, which went hand in hand with the propaganda of progress. In the nineteenth century, progress was called the "great movement." Thus, the heroizing of progress and speed is a phenomenon related to the beginnings of both advertisement and the need for publicity. The first posters of the French railroad and the paintings in the train stations were publicity for transportation. I remember frescoes showing a departing train with beaches and harbors on the horizon. In some stations, there were paintings representing seaside resorts. This was a kind of social advertisement for leisure activities.

Does that mean that there is a complicity between this progress of speed and the image of the world that we create for ourselves? Reading your work, I get the

impression that there is a connection between speed and what you call "the vision machine."[10]

Speed enables you to see. It does not simply allow you to arrive at your destination more quickly, rather it enables you to see and to foresee. To see, yesterday with photography and cinema, and to foresee today with electronics, the calculator and the computer. Speed changes the world vision. In the nineteenth century, with photography and cinema, world vision becomes "objective." (The word "objective"[11] appears not only in the camera but also in philosophical and political thought.) It can be said that today, vision is becoming "teleobjective." That is to say that television and multimedia are collapsing the close shots of time and space as a photograph collapses the horizon in the telephotographic lens. Thus, speed enables you to see differently, and it is beginning with the nineteenth century that this world vision changes and public space becomes a public image through photography, cinematography and television.

What do you mean by "world vision?"

I'm using the German term *Weltanschauung*, which to me seems very important and evocative.

The term "world vision" could just as easily be replaced by the term "world perception." Could you expand on this idea of perception? Philosophers would say that there is a perceptive *a priori* in your work...

That's true, I would have trouble denying it...

How do you justify the importance that you give to perception?

I was a follower of *Gestalttheorie*, I audited Maurice Merleau–Ponty's lectures[12] and I made paintings. So I am a man of the *percept* as well as the concept — without, however, being Berkeleyan. The great break of the nineteenth century, along with the transportation revolution, was the advent of an aesthetics of disappearance which followed the aesthetics of appearance.

The aesthetics of appearance concerns both sculpture and painting. Forms emerge from their material — marble for a Michelangelo sculpture, canvas for a Leonardo da Vinci painting — and the persistence of the support is the essence of the advent of the image, the very image that emerges by way of the sketch and that is fixed with a varnish, just as marble is polished.

With Niepce and Daguerre, an aesthetics of disappearance was born. Through the invention of the instant photo that made the cinematographic photogram possible, the aesthetics was set in motion. Things exist even more so because they disappear. Film is an aesthetics of disappearance staged by sequences. It is no longer a question of transportation, it is the speed of the snapshot, then the speed of twenty–four images per second of film that will revolutionize perception and completely change the aesthetics. Confronted with the aesthetics of disappearance, all that remains is retinal persistence. Retinal persistence is necessary to see the images of the sequence, or the photogram, come to life. So, we move from the persistence of a material — marble or the painter's canvas — to the cognitive persistence of vision. It is the possibility to take snapshots, in other words to accelerate the shooting process, which favored the appearance of an aesthetics of disappearance that continues today in television and video.

If we consider on the one hand Cézanne, who said that by painting apples he tried to translate "the appleness of the apple," and on the other hand, a photograph by Doisneau, which shows the "what has been" that Roland Barthes spoke about,[13] what difference do you see between a nineteenth century painting and a snapshot?

In my opinion, the two are related; you cannot separate a drawing by Rodin — his drawings are animated, they are already cinematic — a photograph and a nineteenth century painting. Cézanne and the Impressionists would have been impossible without the invention of the photograph, that is to say without the negation of a mode of representation of the world which was monopolized by the photograph. "Realism," objectivism, photographic objectivity all caused the great painters to diverge.

You mean to say that their work in painting is a form of resistance to photography?

Absolutely. A divergence occurred. Seurat and pointillism, then Signac; the impressionists, Cézanne, Monet... were an initial divergence with respect to the appearance of the photographic cliché. Their reality, or the way they painted, was already determined by a resistance to reality. Reality diverged, it was no longer exactly what it had been. It is impossible to separate the phenomena of perception that succeeded one another during that period. Rodin made animated drawings and not simply the drawings of a sculptor, because he was a man of modeling, a man of plaster. He understood very well that the question of the speed with which one models a volume is more important than volume itself. Plaster is not a noble material, it is not a Michelangelo. Rodin was as efficient in his plasters that he shaped with his fingers at an extraordinary speed as he was in his incredible drawings of nudes which, by the way, could be likened to photograms — Rodin was already in the era of photocinematography. Photography and cinematography cannot be separated. Pairs have formed and painting has diverged all the way to abstraction, even to disappearance... Now, both painting and drawing are disappearing, just as writing risks disappearing behind multimedia.

Is it always possible to diverge?

In my opinion, yes, in the order of relative speeds. It is in human nature to resist. André Malraux said: "You are human when you can say no." I believe that now would be a good time to remember that. In short, I think that divergence, the resistance of the nineteenth-century painters, is extraordinary, and it is also a lesson for writers. Joyce, Beckett and Kafka were writers who diverged writing.

Let's come back to the image. One of the strong points of your analysis concerns WWII and the documentary school. According to you, wartime filmmakers

“

The battlefield
is the field
of perception.

”

aren't merely witnesses, they anticipate the world to come. Can you clarify this idea?

War reveals with immediacy that every battle and every conflict is a field of perception.

The battle field is first a field of perception. Seeing them coming and knowing that they are going to attack are determining elements of survival. In war, you can't be surprised, for surprise is death. The 1914 war and WWII radically modified the field of perception. Before WWI, war was always waged with maps. Yves Lacoste[14] said: "Geography is meant to wage war." It happens that maps are drawn using topographical landmarks or surveys to direct artillery firing. If the 1914 war was not a total war, then at least it had totalitarian tendencies, and it destroyed all the topographical landmarks of eastern France. Thus, after every artillery battle, it was absolutely imperative to make photo-mosaics in order to get reoriented and not massacre each other needlessly. The first planes were used not to fight but to observe from above, as the first balloons were used to photograph the enemy lines. So, the cinema, the photo–cinema, the photo–mosaic and the documentary were all used to wage war and favored an expanded vision of the battle field. In the past, in order to see the enemy, you had to climb a high point or a watchtower and then you could see them coming. Later, the plane and camera were used to try and locate the enemy.

Thus, WWI was a revolution in perception, and much earlier than Dziga Vertov — remember that *The Man with the Camera* dates back to 1929 and that the news cars that Dziga Vertov launched in 1921 were already being used to wage war five or six years prior. Civilians were forbidden to photograph or film the war — with the exception of Griffith — but on the other hand, the photography invented by Niepce and Daguerre was being used and the first cameras were used to film the battle fields. Jean Renoir was an aviator and aerial photographer during the 1914 war.

After 1914, war became a war film; there were no longer paintings of battles or maps highlighted in red or blue, but a film.

An edifying film or a propaganda film?

Documentary filmmaking developed mainly in England during WWII, partly thanks to Vertov. Yet, one cannot understand Vertov and *The Man with the Camera* or the documentary filmmaking that originated at that time without going back to the 1914 war.

We also have to talk about the propaganda element. Advertisement, which we talked about in reference to the modes of transportation, very quickly became veritable propaganda that had to be supported by photos. Wartime filmmakers fed it in both camps. This lesson was not forgotten during WWII since it became an ideological war, a war of opinion between the Allies, fascism or Nazism. It is well known that the war of 1939–1945 was a war of radio and cinema. It was a war of aviation and tanks, the *Blitzkrieg* of the tanks invading France, the destruction of Coventry and Rotterdam... But it was also Goebbels's frenzied use of the cinema and radio, which he completely controlled, as well as the use of the latter by the Resistance. Moreover, General de Gaulle said that without the radio, there wouldn't have been French Free Forces. On the one hand, Hitler commanded his generals and his troops by radio-telephone, while on the other he lead his people with radio and newsreels.

People don't realize how much newsreels (those of Mussolini, the Duce, are called *Luce*, the light of Italian fascism) are the same as the evening news on television. That is where politics is played out. Before the fictional film, there were newsreels in which the great *conducatore*, Mussolini, and the Führer both spoke. This is also what appears in theatrical political ceremonies, such as the one in Nuremberg which, before even becoming a propaganda film, was filmed theater, an aesthetic way to do politics. I am thinking of Leni Reifenstahl's *Triumph of the Will* and the nighttime ceremony in the stadium lit by anti-aerial defense projectors. Film then became a battle site and British documentary filmmaking later opposed this tyranny of German newsreels by inventing critical newsreels. First, newsreels having a deliberate simplicity and naiveté, and then critical newsreels, in other words a sort of ethno-cinema that the British developed before the documentary school of American video makers.

So, we have gone from advertisement to propaganda and from propaganda to the occupation of an emotional territory. People who listened to the news on the radio at night — "the French speaking to the French" — lived in a virtual territory which was that of Free France, whereas those who listened to the Führer spitting into his microphone were in another virtual country.

And yet, *Rome, Open City* heralds a renaissance of the cinema. With this film, a "possible world" is

sketched out. Isn't it paradoxical to think that war is at the origin of Italian neo-realism?

This paradox has haunted me since I was born. In my opinion, the key is a line from Hölderlin: "And wherever danger is found, there also grows that which saves." In other words, wherever the greatest danger is found, salvation is also found. Salvation is at the edge of the precipice, and every time you approach danger, you also near salvation. This is the paradox of modern society, and the Italian realism of Rossellini, which I like very much, like the British documentary school, is a sociological or ethnological approach to reality. There again, just as the painters diverged, the filmmakers also diverged. They saw the negative effects of progress and propaganda, which gave rise to the modern press and the current abuses, and they diverged toward a fine, artistic approach, through Rossellini up to the French "new wave." In 1959, *Hiroshima Mon Amour*[15] provoked an upheaval comparable to the one caused by Seurat or Cézanne in the Impressionist period. Art then frees itself from advertisement, from a predigested message. The nature of advertisement is to have a hidden message, while the nature of art is to have none at all if not its own, and that is a great mystery.

So art frees itself from the linear narrative...

And as for its structure, art continues the tradition of Eisenstein, that is to say the art of montage. It works in short sequences because in war one cannot work for a long time. Visions of war are threatening for photographers and filmmakers. At that time, jump cuts were discovered. Maurice Tourneur developed them in the United States, but they were invented by newsreels. Jump cuts are made in newsreels because there is no alternative. There is a presence of risk that implies a halting montage, a montage in which changes in time, shot and point of view prevail and bring about a sort of Cubism in cinema. This is the equivalent of what Cubism was, but this time reality serves as material. There is a fly's eye, the eye of fear, the one of "I am looking away, I have no more time to photograph," etc. We stand before a divergence, and the great cinema that is coming to a close today with Wiseman, Godard, Ken Loach and many others has come out that.

One might say that fear will be transferred into the character.

All the more so since the years 1945–1950 were the years of nuclear deterrence, of the great anxiety which lasted for forty years. I lived that and I have to say that at the time, fear became a mass phenomenon. During the war, there were mass fears concerning the exterminated populations, but they did not last very long — often just the time of a bombing or the seizing of hostages. After 1945–50, the world was afraid of the end of the world. It was the time of nuclear deterrence and halting cinema, the cinema of suspense that was the cinema of anxiety, which is to say of survival. We lived because we were still surviving. We entered another world that was no longer that of the speed of transportation and the speed of communications — with the development of television and the airlines — but that of the atomic age, that is to say the possibility of an end of the world decided by man by way of a total war between the East and the West. *Hiroshima Mon Amour* was the great film of this entry of art into deterrence, and it is unlike any other. It is not only political parties and armies that were deterred. Art was also deterred.

The technological revolution in transportation and communications has also changed our relationship to the machine. There was a time when it was possible to disassemble and reassemble the motor of a machine. Now, with the microprocessor, this process of dissection of the technical tool is no longer feasible. As Gilbert Simondon said, the "mode of existence of technical objects" changed.

Simondon wrote that book in 1957. By its very title, it was a revolution "of the mode of existence of technical objects."[16] We have entered the age of the automaton, not the old myth, but the working robot. The idea that Simondon presented there was one of the ambitions of engineering of that time: to make a motor whose hood would be welded and thus be completely isolated from being. It would be isolated not only from the human–mechanic who assembles or disassembles this motor, but also from the human–pilot, from the human–*conducatore*. In the fifties, and even as early as 1945, the Germans were using the first robots. The V1s were robots having an inertia room that allowed them to direct themselves toward London. Yet, there were also the small radio-controlled Goliath tanks by wire that exploded into the big Sherman tanks. For their part, the Americans instituted telemetry for bombing in 1945. I remember a film about a B17 fortress that takes off completely empty, with pilots guiding it from the ground with a remote control. What is interesting about Simondon is the idea that a technical being emerges next to the living being. There is an inanimate being next to the animated being.

Yes, but this being isn't frightening yet. It can still be relatively controlled.

Not for long. As early as 1952, Norbert Wiener feared that cybernetics, which he invented with Alan Turing and Claude Shannon,[17] would become a threat to democracy. Atomic power is a great revolution, so is computer science, and the men whom I just named are, however, aware that totalitarian control of populations is possible with computer science and robotics, without the necessary political guarantee. Remember that cybernetics — from the Greek *kubernân*: "to direct" — deals with processes of control and communication between men and machines. These two populations, living beings and technical objects, may then come into conflict; and it is the very people who developed the automatons of early cybernetics who alerted the public about the political risks involved. What a perfect example of the critique of technology by its inventors!

Faced with microprocessors and emerging computer science, Simondon thought that it was absolutely necessary to recreate a technical culture, to reconsider the arts in their post-modern version. Wouldn't better teaching of technology be one way to avoid the tyranny of computer science and technology?

We are always confronted with a phenomenon of collaboration or resistance. We have seen this with the diverging painters and filmmakers, and we are seeing it again in the technosciences. Technical culture is a necessity, as artistic culture once was. Unfortunately, this technical culture has not been developed and still remains very much elitist. There is no democratization of this technical culture. Faced with any technical object, whatever it may be, it is once again necessary to diverge. It is necessary to become a critic. Impressionism was a critique of photography, and documentary filmmaking a critique of propaganda. So, today, we have to institute an art criticism of the technosciences in order to make the relation to technology diverge. As an art lover, I can only develop my interest for technology through critique. Only critique can bring about the progress of technical culture. Nothing can be gained without loss. When a technical object is invented, say the elevator, the stairway is lost; when the transatlantic airlines are created, the ocean liner is lost...

...and when the high-speed train is invented, the landscape is lost.

Yes. And it is not being negative to proffer this idea. It means entering a technical culture that would resume the best work done in the Impressionist period or in the period of documentary filmmaking. If we do not see the number of art critics increase in the coming years, there won't be any freedom from multimedia and new technologies. There will be a tyranny of technoscience.

Does this tyranny apply to research? Is there not a bit of phobia in your position? For example, do you give in to the fear of experimentation on human embryos? Does it seem right to you to prohibit such experimentation?

I think that it was right to stop this kind of research, and the atomic engineers who refused to develop the nuclear program in the United States were right as well. However, the question cannot be resolved by stepping back. Neither genetic engineering nor the atom bomb can be uninvented, and nuclear energy even less so. If the task is not to uninvent, then it is at least to surpass. An invention can only be fought with another invention. An idea can only be fought with another idea or another concept. Here, the notion of information is at the center of science and its militarization.

Do you mean to say that the threat of war is an integral part of the technological choice?

We should never forget that the end of WWII resulted in deterrence. We stopped waging war on each other, we prohibited ourselves from doing so, yet we threatened each other more and more through the arms race, the space race and the development of information — satellites, instantaneous communication, Arpanet, which gave rise to the Internet. All of this came out of deterrence, which was only made possible with the creation of a military-industrial complex. Eisenhower set up this military-industrial complex, and when he left the presidency in 1961, he asserted that this complex was dangerous to democracy. He was an expert in logistics, he knew what he was talking about.

It is therefore impossible to understand the development of the sciences and technology without recognizing the absolute threat that the East or the West wanted to weigh on its enemy. And this first military-industrial complex resulted in a second one that was even more threatening, the military-industrial and scientific complex beginning with the Vietnam War and *electronic warfare*. After Vietnam, war has become an essentially electronic phenomenon. Drones, satellites, missile-guiding technologies and neo–atom bombs — like the depression bombs seen during the Gulf War — are all being used. Similarly, information is becoming world–wide. The National Security Agency (NSA) keeps monitoring information and is becoming a sort of Department of World Information. It is collecting information not only on the enemy but also on the world. Thus, it is no longer a militarization of science that is happening, but rather a militarization of information, a militarization of knowledge.

Can one say, though, that the military–industrial complex is at the origin of the Internet?

The Pentagon's latest technologies of war are virtual war technologies, information war technologies. The first *cyberwar* maneuvers occurred in Hohenfeld in the summer of 1995. The site of nuclear war is no longer the arsenal or even an air or space weapons system, but the C3i (Control, Command, Communication, Intelligence), in other words the management of war where all information converges and where everything should be known about everything at every moment. It is the site of a tyranny of information, an example of which being the manipulation of CNN during the Gulf War. According to Einstein, the development of the atom bomb made necessary the development of the computer bomb, the bomb of totalitarian information. The total war of 1939–1945 resulted in total peace with deterrence and, thus, in almost cybernetic control of the enemy.

The Internet is the product of the Pentagon, and all the satellite technologies were initially military. They achieved the militarization of knowledge, which is an unthinkable phenomenon. The militarization of science with the military-scientific complex and the militarization of all information with the military-informational complex confront us with a phenomenon of totalitarianism that has never existed before.

However, not all scientists are subject to this complex. The researcher who works at the Pasteur Institute or the one who works on the brain at Jussieu is not subject to any pressure, even if this research is linked to an economic power. What do you think about the status of scientific inventiveness in relation to technology?

The status of research cannot be opposed by the militarization of science, otherwise it would be cutting it off from its source, which is absolutely inconceivable. Simply stated, a divergence must be invented. This time it is up to scientists to invent an Impressionism, a Cubism and a documentary school on a par with the threat. The threat of realism imposed on the painter or filmmaker by the camera forced them to be innovative, and this innovation allowed an equilibrium to be restored, a common culture, not to mention democratization. The poets, painters and filmmakers were men of divergence. The problem is knowing whether the scientists can also be. They have been put in the same position as the poets faced with Nazism — I'm thinking of Paul Celan or Garcia Lorca. The problem is knowing whether they understood it or not. Apart from a few geneticists and electronics engineers, it seems to me that not many of them are willing to diverge. They are playing the fatal game of negativity.

The loss of the world, or, how to retrieve the body proper

**The loss of
the world,
or, how to
retrieve
the body
proper**

II

The Loss of the World, or, How to Retrieve the Body Proper

What fundamentally distinguishes your conception of time from that of philosophers such as Paul Ricoeur and Gilles Deleuze?

Ricoeur and Deleuze are philosophers, whereas I am an urbanist. I'm not saying that to be modest, because philosophy was born in the city, not in the swamps, in the middle of the ocean or in the mountains. I am a man of the city, and the question of time and the inscription of this time in a given place happens in the city. Saint Augustine's *The City of God*, in a way, is an urbanist book; not a book of sacred urbanism, but simply a book of urbanism. Without the city, there can be no politics. Without the history of the city, there is no reality of history. The city is the major political form of history. My work deals not only with the narrative, but also with the trajectory. This is perhaps where I differ from Ricoeur, but not with Deleuze. I do not work on the subject and object — that is the work of the philosopher — but rather on the "traject." I have even proposed to inscribe the trajectory between the subject and the object to create the neologism "trajective," in addition to "subjective" and "objective." I am thus a man of the trajective, and the city is the site of trajectories and trajectivity. It is the site of proximity between men, the site of organization of contact. Citizenship is the organization of trajectories between groups, between men, between sects, etc. When it is said that citizenship is related to blood and soil, once again the trajectory is forgotten, that is to say the nature of the proximity that holds human beings together in the city. Immediate proximity with the agora, forum and church; metabolic proximity with the horse; mechanical proximity with the train and the transportation revolution; and finally, electromagnetic proximity with globalization and real time that prevails over real space. All of history has been an urbanization of the real space of the town, the city, the capital, the metropolis and, today, the megalopolis. We have witnessed the tragic results of this in the suburbs... When the city becomes too big, catastrophic urbanization becomes apparent.

Yet, in spite of the Internet and the information superhighway, we have not asked ourselves if it is possible to urbanize real time, if the virtual city is a possibility. If the answer is no, then a general accident is inevitable, the accident of history, the accident of accidents that Epicurus spoke of regarding history. If we are not capable of urbanizing the real time of exchange, in other words the *live* city-world, the city-world in real time, through the globalization of telecommunications, then both history and politics will be called into question. This is an extraordinary drama. I'm not saying that it's inevitable, I'm simply asking the question.

You cite Saint Augustine; do you mean that refiguration of human time is only possible from the moment that the city exists in its major political form? Ricoeur would then be sinning by idealism?

Absolutely. I am a man of the form–city, a formalist, because I am above all an urbanist. Urbanism has been heavily criticized as formalism because it gave form to societies — we have seen the results of this in high-density housing developments — but let's not forget Venice, Naples, Bologna and the marvelous cities of the Middle Ages. Two questions come up: first, will there be a cyber-*città* after the cine-*città* and the tele-*città*? If the answer is no, then is it over? *Finita la commedià,* as the Italians would say. Next, is form still possible when the site is lost? Can the *hic et nunc* survive when the *dasein* is lost? When it is lost for oneself, it is also lost for the other.

A threat is emerging that fulfills Nietzsche's hope opposing Christ's words by inverting them — namely *love thy distant neighbor as yourself.* The question of neighbor and distant neighbor is essentially the question of the city. The neighbor is the one next to me and with whom I make up the city and defend city rights. For all practical purposes, those who are outside of the city are foreigners or enemies, and today the question of loss arises again. Love your distant neighbor, meaning foreigner, yes! but love your distant neighbor to the detriment of your neighbor, no!

So you aren't very cosmopolitan...

I am a "citizen of the world." I don't wish for the return of nationalism, but if tomorrow we love only our distant neighbor without being conscious of hating our neighbors because they're present, because they smell, because they're noisy, they bother me and they summon me, unlike my distant neighbor whom I can zap..., so, if tomorrow we start preferring our distant neighbor at the expense of our neighbor, then we would be destroying the city, city rights.

As for this reduction of distances, you write in *Open Sky*,[18] "measure is in my soul." Could you explain what you mean by this?

The world is inside of us before being outside of us. Yet, if it is truly outside, in geography and the space–world, then it is also outside through my consciousness of the world. Since I travel and am animated, this awareness of the world is my movement and the nature of my movement. An individual who lives shut up in a place with limited horizons, like many peasants of the Middle Ages, does not have the same consciousness of the world as someone who travels to the other side of the world in a few hours. *Mental–mapping* evolves with the transportation revolution and the communication revolution. The faster I travel to the end of the world, the faster I come back, and the emptier my mental–map becomes. Going to Tokyo in the same time it takes to get to Naples by train has permanently reduced my world. I can no longer have the mental vision of the world that I had before going to Tokyo in fourteen hours. When I then gave a teleconference in Tokyo with eight hours of jetlag some time after that, my mental map experienced another shrinking that was just as permanent.

The measure of the world is our freedom. Knowing that the world around us is vast, being aware of this, is an element of human freedom and greatness, even if we don't take advantage of it. Howard Hughes, who experienced traveling around the world in a few hours, reached a state of mental inertia and loss of relation to the world. This had a pathological effect on him. He was a planet–man who identified the world with his body to the point of not wanting to leave his *desert inn*, the Las Vegas hotel, and then died like a mental patient...[19]

The threat, and this is the great confinement, is having in one's head a reduced mental picture of the Earth — an Earth that is constantly flown over, traversed and violated in its real size. That shrinking Earth is destroying me for that very reason, me, the planet–man who is no longer aware of any expanse at all. Many astronauts who orbited the Earth have experienced a sort of vertigo in their own relation to themselves. The conquest of space was an experiment on the delirium of losing the Earth — not the end of the Earth, but rather a loss of the mind.

In your work, the question of city rights and that of the loss of the Earth are inseparable from the question of the body proper, namely a body situated in space and time. Could you expand on this idea which I find essential?

The question of corporeality touches us all — and I use the word "touch" intentionally. There are three bodies that are eminently connected: the territorial body, that of the planet and ecology; the social body; and finally, the animal or human body. From this results the need to reorient oneself with respect to the body, to reorient one's body with respect to the other — the question of the neighbor and alterity — but also with respect to the Earth, or the world proper. There cannot be a body proper without a world proper, without a proper orientation. The body proper is oriented with respect to the other, whether woman, friend, enemy... but it is also oriented with respect to the world proper. It is "here and now," *hic et nunc*, it is *in situ*. Being is being present here and now.

The question of telepresence delocalizes the position or orientation of the body. The whole problem of virtual reality is that it essentially denies the *hic et nunc*, it denies the "here" in favor of the "now." I already said that "here" no longer exists, everything is "now"! Reappropriating the body is not merely a question of choreography, of which dance represents the maximum resistance, but also a question of sociography, of relating to others and to the world. Otherwise it's madness, or the loss of both the world and the body. The technological time–gap producing telepresence is trying to make us permanently lose the body proper in favor of excessive love for the virtual body, for this specter that appears in the "strange window" and in the "space of virtual reality." The loss of the other, or the decline of physical presence in favor of an immaterial and ghostly presence, represents a considerable threat.

Jean-Luc Godard said that the Houphouët-Boigny cathedral[20] was already a synthetic product. Couldn't it be said that Patrick Poivre d'Arvor[21] is already a synthetic product? I mean that before even falling into the virtual he's getting ready to do so!

I would go even further, beyond television and its setting, it is the entire city that is falling into the virtual and taking with it individuals who are getting ready to live there. The city has always been a theatrical device with the agora, the church, the forum, the parade ground, etc. Simply put, it was a place where you could gather together, a public space. Today, however, the television setting is replacing public space with public image, and the public image is decentered from the city. The public image is no longer in the city, but rather in the "tele–*città*," already a virtual city, in which we claim to co–habitate because we watch the evening news together. I believe that what is in question behind the problem of virtual space is the loss of the real city. I am an urbanist, and for me, the real city is the site of the social body, the populating site. Today, 80% of the French population is distributed over 20% of the territory, and tomorrow it will reach 90%. Furthermore, the city is attracting its population on the world scale. Thus, a sort of city of cities is being created: the telecommunications city, the Internet city. Next to the virtual bubble of market economy, generated by the *Trading* program and by automatic stock quotations, a virtual urban bubble is forming in which public space has been definitively supplanted by public image. The propaganda about the Internet and the information superhighway aims to urbanize real time at a time when real space is being deurbanized. Our cities, not only São Paulo or Calcutta, but also Washington and the Parisian suburbs, are in an utterly catastrophic situation: they are currently on the verge of implosion. There is a trend toward disintegration of the community made by those who are present in favor of those who are absent, absent because they are connected to the Internet or multimedia. This is an unprecedented event and one of the signs of a general accident. The fact of being closer to someone who is far away than to someone who is right next to you is a phenomenon of political dissolution that affects the entire human race. It is evident that the loss of the body proper is bringing about the loss of the other's body, in favor of a sort of spectrality of the distant neighbor, the one living in the virtual space of the Internet or in the window of the television.

In the case of television, isn't it necessary to make a distinction between the transmitter and the receiver? Isn't it conceivable to invent another television?

To some extent, this is already true. I would say that television is already dead with the advent of multimedia. It is clear that interactivity is the end of television. I would like to say that the example of television is already outdated. Just as photography gave rise to cinematography, video and television are today giving rise to infography. Television is already a surviving form of media.

According to you, was it justified for Daniel Schneiderman to dedicate his program "Arrêt sur images" ("Freeze on Images") to the murder of Khaled Kelkal?[22]

In my opinion, we are in the same situation as in WWII: this endlessly reproduced image is no longer a piece of information but a suggestion, a subjugation of the viewer. Showing an execution once is one thing, it's information, but re-presenting or reproducing it is equivalent to autosuggestion. In other words, we are doing something else than showing reality.

But this program is also meant to reflect upon this image. Does the didactic function of such a project seem convincing to you?

I think that the drilling of the gaze by television has gone so far that it is no longer possible to straighten out the situation in one hour. That being said, I am not opposed to showing catastrophes or accidents, because I believe a museum of accidents is necessary. (On this subject, remember that the tape of the Rodney King affair has been put in a museum.) However, I think that television has become the advertising or propaganda medium *par excellence*. We saw this during the Gulf War, with Timisoara,[23] and we see it every day. Honestly, I am beginning to give up on television. I can no longer tolerate this kind of drilling. It would take the invention of another kind of television, but I believe it's too late. I think that there will be innovation within the new medium but not in the old one. The old medium has gone all the way to the end, which is to say to *its* end. In my opinion, television is gone, but not video.

Aren't you being a bit apocalyptic? Are we so compelled to surrender to the technological environment? Are we bound to perish?

I have no ready-made solutions because these situations are way beyond us. What I can say is that we cannot lose our relation to the body indefinitely, to physical corporeality, let alone physiological corporeality, and we cannot afford to lose the relation of the body to the world because of telecommunication. I think we have reached a limit. I think that the achievement of absolute speed infinitely confines us within the world. The world is shrinking and a feeling of incarceration is already looming, although it is perhaps not yet felt by young people. Foucault's great confinement does not date back to the sixteenth century, but to the twenty-first. It is obvious that once interactivity becomes unlimited, once we can travel to Tokyo in two hours on supersonic planes, then the feeling of the world's narrowness will soon become intolerable. We will have lost the real size of nature. Just as there is pollution of nature, there is pollution of the real size of nature. This is an *intolerable* event. Losing one's body through autism or schizophrenia is equally intolerable. I believe that the new technologies are responsible for the loss of both the body proper in favor of the spectral body, and the world proper in favor of a virtual world. The main question is to regain contact. I said earlier that any acquisition involves a loss. Since the world is a limited space, there comes a day when the losses become intolerable and there are no more benefits. The twenty-first century will probably be the century of this discovery: the losses will outnumber the benefits. We will have to compensate for the loss of the world proper and the loss of the body proper, since, by that time, the situation will have become intolerable for everyone; not only for the poor who find themselves in an impossible situation, an unbelievable repression, both in under–developed countries and in our own, but for the rich as well: seaside resorts were a discovery of the sea, while the jet-set represents a wasting away of the world. The rediscovery of touch, contact through walking and mountain climbing and navigation (Gérard d'Aboville the oarsman is a kind of prophet), these are all signs of another divergence, of a return to the physical, to matter — the signs of a rematerializaton of the body and of the world.

Since terrestrial space has been stolen from us, isn't a glorious escape toward heaven imaginable?

That has been one of the hopes of deterrence. After the air conquest which made WWII possible, the space conquest has made deterrence possible. The Americans dominated space to such an extent that the Berlin wall came down and a kind of peace was recovered beyond deterrence. To some extent, the escape into space was also a loss of Mother Earth, a loss of the body proper, a temptation to colonize other planets or satellites. "He who says great colony says great navy." He who says extraterrestrial colony says great astronautics! I think that today this illusion has been dispelled. *Apollo 13* was not a chance accident — accidents are not heroized. I find that quite positive. I've read the memoirs of the astronaut, Jim Lowell. The crew was about to miss the Earth because they didn't have enough energy to power the ship and reach the necessary return orbit. The astronaut asked his colleagues the following question: the jets will only work one more time and that might not be enough to reach the orbit necessary to get back, what do you think we should do? They all answered: we'd rather

“

My work is that of a limited man who must deal with a limitless situation.

”

burn up in the outer layers of the atmosphere and return to Earth all charred, than drift away into the great cosmic void. I think this choice clearly expresses the necessity not of a return to Earth, but of a return to real space and to the world proper, in other words the body proper, since it would be impossible to separate the body and the world proper.

Isn't this return to the world proper a bit illusory?

My work is that of a limited man who must deal with a limitless situation — a man who started to take an interest in speed when the limit of speed was being reached, three hundred thousand kilometers per second. I cannot conceive of this situation propositionally. I can only say "no."

The problem is the following: is the question of pain after anguish not a current question? No longer the physiological pain in the sense of "I'm in pain," but rather in the sense of a history that would come up against an impasse. The history of my generation has just hit the insurmountable barrier of real time. We broke the two preceding ones, the sound barrier and the heat barrier — the sound barrier with the supersonic plane, and the heat barrier with the stratospheric rocket that makes liberation speed (28,000 km/h) possible and thus allows an individual to be put into orbit. Now, history, our history, has just crashed into the barrier of real time. Everything that I've said in my books about the relationship between politics and speed has reached a limit. From now on, we will not accelerate anymore. From now on, history will have reached its limit speed. This is a question that I cannot answer. However, I do know that this general accident, or the crashing into the time barrier, is an event that will force us to slow down, to regress, or to back up. This regression is a reaction to the attainment of the limit speed. It is still too early to say what form it will take. I cannot provide the solution, but I can say that it will come out of the urban question.

Losing the city, we have lost everything. Recovering the city, we will have gained everything. If there is a solution possible today, it lies in reorganizing the place of communal life. We must not let ourselves be betrayed or fooled by the tele–*città* after the cine–*città.* We must face the drama and tragedy of the city–world, this virtual city that delocalizes work and our relationship to others.

My solution is that of the urbanist in me. Working on the city, we will work on politics as well. In a way, this is a regression, since the word politics comes from *polis*, "city." We crashed into the wall, and we are now returning to the city.

This desire for a return to the city is all to your credit, but don't you think you tend to exaggerate your description of our technological environment?

People might find my approach too negative, but that is not true at all. It's just that I have to do this work on negativity all by myself, whereas most intellectuals have already become collaborators or even advertisers of the technological boom. Some of them even talk about "civilization" through the information technologies. With my work, I am trying to set the record straight. I am not afraid of being a prophet of doom, since there's no one else to do it.

I am passionate about technology myself, and I also know that no territory exists independently of the transportation or communication technologies. This has always been the case, even in the time when people rode donkies. Therefore, my work tries to demonstrate the words of Aesop: "What is the best and worst of things? Information." He actually said "language," but I prefer to say that it's information.

The Internet, the information superhighway and the great holdings that are getting ready to manage the globalization of information are using millions of dollars to flaunt their products. Faced with this, I can only don Cassandra's mask in order to show the hidden side of this technology, its negativity.

You use the word "drama" to talk about the fusion of the biological and the technological. To what extent do you think that computer–assisted medical attention can be a drama?

The word "drama" is not the same as the word "tragedy." It refers to the living. The third revolution is the transplant revolution, the colonization of the body by biotechnology, and thus only the term drama can be used, because it affects the living. Cloning is drama of the living. The fact of receiving pacemakers or additional memory in the body or the brain is drama. Before exploring the question of biotechnologies, however, I would like to underline the fact that to my mind, the word "dramaturgy" is the opposite of the word "thaumaturgy." A thaumaturgist is someone who performs miracles or at least claims to. Today, all the thaumaturgists are calling any technical object a miracle, whether it be the beeper, the Internet or a micro–computer with voice recognition. Thaumaturgical kings are numerous, and no one is denouncing them. The only one opposing the thaumaturgists is the dramatist, or the one who is against the event but wants to show his drama, to reveal that something is being lost.

Nothing is gained without loss. There is no technological gain without loss on the level of the living, the vital. What is true of space that is diminished and reduced to nothing is true of memory. Additional memories are being developed, dead memories that will not only complete but also replace the living memory of humans. Biotechnology is the next aspect of the technological revolution. After the communication revolution, the attainment of absolute speed and the reduction of the world to nothing, we are heading toward the latest threat, namely the reduction of the living to less than nothing — in other words, the artificial insertion of micro–technological objects into the body foreshadowed by pacemakers. Now you will tell me that pacemakers save people from dying. Of course they do. I have friends who have had heart transplants and some of them have pacemakers, so I have nothing to say against transplants that save lives. However, certain technologies sometimes become life–support technologies and then become rivals. When Marvin Minsky[24] claims that tomorrow miniature computers will be able to help an individual's memory, it is no longer a question of therapy but that of the prosthetic–man. Technology is colonizing the human body just as it colonized the body of the Earth. The highways, railways and airlines have colonized the territorial body by organizing it. Today, it is the animal body that is being threatened with colonization by micromachines.

Can you explain the term miniaturization?

Miniaturization is a dwarfing effect that concerns both the medium and its object. The new transportation technologies — the Concord, supersonic planes, the high–speed train — reduce and miniaturize the distances of the territorial body, in other words of the environment. The miniaturization of technical objects, known as nanotechnologies, is the ability to create micromachines capable of merging with our organs. This technology will not miniaturize the human body, but rather its properties. It will reduce the properties of the living under the pretext of completing and assisting them. It's the myth of the bionic man, of the Nietzschean *Superman.*

You make a connection between the body of the Earth and the living body. In your opinion, this question regarding the body of the Earth is related to the death of geography, or the loss of travel and the tangible experience of movement within the corporeal space. Doesn't this loss of geography go hand in hand with a loss of history?

Certainly, history and geography have been simultaneously determined by two major historical and geographical intervals: the space interval and the time interval. We have just invented a third interval, the light–type or zero sign interval, in other words the interval that results from the speed of light.

First, it abolishes the space interval, that expanse that made borders and cadastres, that distributed populations throughout the world with *no man's lands* and geographical organization. It also abolishes the time interval that has made history. Calendars, ephemerides and clocks have been the basis of history. There is a temporal historical foundation at the root of the history of mankind. This organization of clocks that separates the life of mankind into different periods and different nations is annihilated by the instantaneity of the third light–type interval that cancels both the time and space intervals. This is an unprecedented event.

This loss of the expanse of real space in favor of real time is a kind of attack on the real size of nature. Not only is there an attack against nature by the pollution of substances, but also an attack against the real size of nature by the pollution of distances. Behind globalization there is something developing that Foucault analyzed for the eighteenth century: *the great confinement*. This great confinement is before us. It resides in this absence of geographical space and this absence of delay in communication which determined human freedom. Remember that one of the most important liberties is the freedom to move.

This freedom is not threatened by a prohibition as in Foucault's time, when people were locked up in jail so they could no longer move. Jean Giono used to make his schoolmaster say: "Children, don't run in the courtyard, it will seem bigger."

Isn't it contradictory to claim that there is a loss of history in light of what happened in the former Yugoslavia and in Chechenya?

The word "loss" does not mean the same as "end." I am not like Fukuyama. I am not evoking the end of geography or the end of history. I take "loss" to mean "relativization." Since relativity, speed is absolute and is a limit on human activity. The loss of history means that the immediacy of the present prevails over the past and the future. So the possibility of a "presentified" history emerges, one known as current events or *news*. There again is the considerable importance of the communication revolution and the power of the media. History only happens in the present. Today, historians are being pushed around by the media. Everyone doing serious work in history must work on the media, except that this work has nothing to do with the old chronicler's work. Today's chronicles are predigested matter in which information is abridged as much as possible.

History has been created through stories and the memories of individuals having witnessed certain events. Today, however, the media no longer exists as narratives but rather as flashes and images. History is therefore being reduced to images.

In your latest book, you talk a lot about gray ecology and dromospheric ecological pollution. Why does the pollution of distances seem even more harmful to you than that of substances?

This expression refers to the color green. Green ecology is the ecology of substances, in other words the pollution of the flora and fauna, the atmosphere, the hydrosphere, etc. Now, aside from this green ecology represent-

“

I talk about dromospheric pollution. Speed pollutes the distances of the world.

”

ing the pollution of nature, there is also a gray ecology. Not only does the word "gray" mean a lack of color, but it also refers to Hegel's gray ontology. Aside from this visible pollution that is very material, concrete and substantial, there is also an ecology of distances. Pollution includes the pollution of nature's real size by speed. That is why I talk about dromospheric pollution. Speed pollutes the expanse of the world and the distances of the world. This ecology cannot be perceived because it is mental, not visible.

In the past, travel was made up of three parts: departure, itinerary and arrival. Today, generalized arrival has prevailed over all departures. The feeling of confinement in the world can only increase because "achievement is a limit" — second Aristotelian axiom. Soon, we are going to experience the end of the world — not the apocalyptic end of the world, but the world as finite. Paul Valéry said, "The time of the finite world is beginning." Today, it's the space of finite time that is beginning. The dramatic event of this confinement is that youth can no longer conquer the world. "Travel forms youth," as the saying goes. When a son is encouraged to travel in the world, he is sent into the world. If, as a child, the world's distance is lost and reduced to nothing, then one experiences a feeling of incarceration and travel no longer forms youth. Youth will be born into a closed world representing an unparalleled threat.

The Earth will still have a circumference of 40,000 kilometers, but it will not be traveled anymore. Let me return to the example of the elevator and the staircase. When a staircase goes up to the tenth floor and next to it there is an elevator, the staircase is lost and everyone takes the elevator. In this case, it is no longer a question of a building but rather of the world that surrounds us. It is hard to imagine this situation of confinement for the coming generations. This loss of real space has already occurred in the conquest of space. The conquest of space in the 1960s was the result of the fight between the East and the West to conquer orbital space. That was already a symptom of this confinement, in a world reduced to nothing.

In 1978, you wrote *Popular Defense and Ecological Struggles*.[24] What has changed since then in your critique of industrial society and the harm it causes? Does gray ecology still depend on popular movements in order to fight?

The type of resistance was outlined in *Speed and Politics*[25] which had prefaced *Popular Defense and Ecological Struggles*, The history of politics is inseparable from the history of wealth and capital — you don't have to be Marxist to say that. Acceleration is the hidden side of wealth and accumulation, or capitalization: in the past, the acceleration of maritime transportation, today, the acceleration of information. Therefore, a politics of speed is imperative. When telecommunication, the Internet or the automatization of interactivity are threatening us with social cybernetics, there must be a political economy of speed, just as there is a political economy of wealth and accumulation. Otherwise we won't be able to resist this pollution of distances that is both intangible and invisible.

Take the example of the Atlantic. It's just a big garbage can now. With the invention of supersonic planes, cruise ships were eradicated. Now the Atlantic is only used by a few transporter or cargo ships. It is no longer traveled by man, except as a playing field for solitary crossings or oarsmen like Aboville. There has been a loss in size of the Atlantic that foreshadows the loss in size of the planet.

So many losses! Not even sex is safe. With cybersex, it, too, is disappearing, and, as you say, it has been replaced by fear. What do sex and love mean for you, Paul Virilio?

Fear of the other is the very opposite of love. It's easy to forget that when one thinks of love in terms of eroticism, sexuality and the pleasures of the flesh. The question of love is the opposite of hate, or the fear of others. Hatred is born out of fear. Today we are witnessing a disintegration of the populating unit. For the people of the city, the populating unit represents the family and the populating site represents the city. The larger the populating site, the smaller the populating unit.

Ancient cities are the tribes of Israel. In the Middle Ages, they were formed by extended families, as is the case in Africa today. In the sixteenth and seventeenth centuries, the bourgeois family began to predominate with the parents, grandparents and children. Then came the nuclear family with the Industrial Revolution. And today, in the metacity — or the virtual city — we have the single parent family. The family line no longer exists, the family disintegrates. The woman or the man leaves with the children. We have therefore reached the end of a cycle, or the beginning of a reciprocal exclusion. Divorce is not merely a phenomenon of mores, but a phenomenon of the human race, and teletechnologies highlight this. Telesexuality (or cybersexuality) comes on top of events that were already cataclysmic. To demonstrate that this has nothing to do with any kind of morality, but is instead related to demography, let me take an example: Flaubert's or Maupassant's prostitute, the one from *The Tellier House*, is a woman that you are friends with. In today's cities, the prostitute is the girl in the shop window! It's very much a product. If you consider the striptease or the *peepshow*, there is no fear of the other, but a retreat or distancing; with video-pornography, for example, this distance is at its height. And with the pink Minitel,[26] there is only a voice — the Minitel is used for more than just making dates — there's the telephone for that. Now, we have cybersex and telesexuality in which divorce is at its height because we are splitting up. It is no longer a couple divorcing, but rather a divorce of copulation! Furthermore, the expression "making love from a distance" reflects Nietzsche's words: "Love thy distant neighbor as thyself." All the insanity surrounding sexual harassment, this attack on someone else's intentions, is a truly pathological sign of the hatred of one's neighbor, male or female. This is the end of sexual alterity and the madness of the race generated by developed nations.

Is it true that you found a text on cyberfeminism?

This text is taken from *Chimère*, the journal of Félix Guattari. Cyberfeminism has existed in the United States for a while now, and it seeks to find its place in the control of sensations. In order to understand this, we must return to cybersexuality which is on the rise because the individual senses have been transferred to a remote place. Some 80% of micro–electronic production is made of captors, sensors or teledetectors which have made possible not only tele–hearing, with the radio and the microphone, but also tele–touching with the tele–tactile glove with tension return that allows you to touch and feel the pressure of someone else's hand and even allows you to feel their body against yours with a suit of information or data, a "datasuit" — all this from a distance (from thousands of miles away). The latest captor that has been invented is the odor captor. Now we can smell from a distance! The last sense that cannot be transferred is taste. You can't enjoy a good wine from a distance. Somewhere there is a disconnecting, a way of leaving the body of sensations...

You seem sensitive to the problem of the increase in the rate of divorce. Do you consider reconstructed families to be new families?

Yes. Besides, there are reconstructed families in every family. The reconstructed family is in a way a self-defense invention in reaction to the trend which I have just described. There are two laws of urbanism: the first is the perseverance of the site. A city can never be rebuilt somewhere else. The second is that the more the populating site expands, the more the populating unit falls apart. Even in Africa, where demography is always growing, it is nonetheless falling in the cities... In Western countries, this law has reached a state of crisis with single parent families. Since winter 1994, mothers have been living underneath Paris with their children. They have to hide so that the authorities don't take their children away from them. This is an image of the drama of our societies.

Isn't this trend toward the separation of the sexes which you describe counterbalanced in Europe by a cultural durability of the courtly model?

It's not impossible, but the point of my work is rather to expose the negative trends in order to preempt harm. My work is statistical, I anticipate trends that can already be observed. I don't deny that these are only tendencies, and that there are also stable families and a steady demographic procreation. Yet, if we want this to continue, we must denounce negativity and the tendency toward exclusion of both the poorest people and the other. This exclusion is exacerbated by the teletechnologies and by long–distance work that foreshadows long–distance love.

As for divorce, I think there is a problem of temporality. Consider the way people lived in the last century. The life that a couple led was completely different from that of a contemporary couple. The pressure of the city, the rapidity of exchanges, the stress and acceleration of mores all contribute to the fact that in five years, a modern couple has lived the equivalent of fifty years of a couple in the nineteenth century. So, having lived fifty years in five years, they can no longer stand to live together... These are phenomena of "tempo." There is a rhythmology to public life. People can get along at a certain rhythm, but if this rhythm is accelerated, they snap. The submarine and the factory are good examples: in the submarine, the law of proximity of the crew throws everyone on top of one another. Hatred results, because the necessary distance is missing. In the factory, with the high volume of work in addition to the clock and productivity, people end up hating those that they would have liked under less frantic working conditions. What Jacques Derrida would call the excessive tempo of the modern city is an aspect of the disintegration and the deconstruction of the populating unit. The result of this is a sort of cold civil war.

How can we control this tempo, which is destroying relations in couples and neighborhoods, in order to create a dignified life in spite of all this?

By taking back language. Here again we find the words of Aesop. Language is the worst of things and the best of things. This paradox is at the heart of the information revolution. Taking back language means talking with one another. Media information prevents us from doing this, and this is quite evident in the suburbs. Why is there violence? Because we no longer talk to one another... In order to take back language, we have to abandon certain types of activities. I don't want to use myself as an example, because I believe there are many others, but now I don't have a car or a fax machine, I don't watch television anymore, and I rarely listen to the radio; which means I'm reading again. When you deny yourself reading and writing, you deny yourself language and, thus, contact with others. Socialization occurs with language, with languages. The best way to love one another is through language. This social necessity is largely threatened by the information technologies.

You are afraid of the smart house, domotics, telework, you condemn home use of the computer which reduces learning and discovery time. Can't these tools be used judiciously in the classroom?

Of course they can. Last year, in my institution, the Special School of Architecture of Paris, I began a multi–year investment for its general computerization. But the question of domotics is related to both the question of inhabited space or the habitation — "house," "dwelling" — and that of the relation to the body of the inhabitant. Through Le Corbusier and all the ancients, there was a relation to the body which was that of the *modulor*. The human body is the reference for its habitat. The ergonomic dimension of the body must be taken into consideration in the habitat. However, the new technologies make habitation possible without moving. With domotics, it's not television channels that are zapped but rather the lights, the heat, and the opening of the shutters. You don't have to go to the window to open it, just zap it. So there is a kind of reference to a handicapped body and no longer to a locomotive body. The overequipped able–body of domotics, the one that experiences *home automation*, is the equivalent of the equipped invalid. I took part in an exposition at La Villette for the handicapped called "The Repaired Man." I was surprised to see that these men in their little cars were scandalized by the teletechnologies. I saw reactions of astonishment to the fact that able–bodied people use technologies meant for invalids who suffer, for example, from not being able to move in order to open a window.

Today, the telesurveillance screen is beginning to replace the window. A videosurveillance screen can replace a window without drilling into a wall. In supersonic planes, the windows will be replaced with videos. The pilots will see the landscape through video, and this is what is happening now in our relation to the outside world. In the past, if you wanted to know what temperature it was, you looked out the window and saw if it was nice out or not. Today, you turn on the television to get the news and the weather. Yet, what's more, in 1995, thanks to the teletechnologies, the virtual portal was invented. After the virtual window — the telesurveillance screen — the impossible was invented, the virtual vestibule, the virtual entrance!

What is that?

It's a calling room where you invite the specter or clone of your visitor.

Could you give an example?

A vestibule is a semi–private or semi–public room. When people knock, they are either let in or not. It is thus a quasi–virtual transition room next to the dining room, a warm room where guests are greeted. With the datasuit or the visiohelmet, a kind of virtual vestibule is perfected, known as a virtual portal. If two individuals are equipped with this device, they can meet from a distance by electromagnetic transmission. Physically, the portal rings, some one tele–arrives, then you have to put on your datasuit and enter this calling room in order to see, hear and touch your visitor, all via an interposed clone. You will feel the sensations of the other person's body, knowing that they are in New York, for example, in their vestibule. And they will, of course, have the same sensations. It's a sort of home teleport. Domotics, or "immotics" — the domotized *immeuble,* or apartment building — results in not only the disappearance of the city, but also the disappearance of architecture as a structuring element of the way we relate to others. The arrival of this clone is nothing like the arrival of a woman or a man at your place. And then you can zap it... For the urbanist in me, these images are catastrophic from the point of view of both politics and our relation to others.

A few good reasons to start resisting

A few good reasons to start resisting

"

The city/country opposition shaped the nineteenth century, and the city center/ suburb opposition shaped the twentieth. We are currently living this very latest opposition.

"

III

A Few Good Reasons to Start Resisting

An op–ed column in the November 4, 1995 issue of *Le Monde* reads as follows: "The reality of the nineteenth century continues to pervade the image that many French people have of their city on the eve of the twenty-first century. They think that France is still a rural country, while the majority of its inhabitants live in the cities." Do you agree with the idea that we are still living a largely rural fantasy?

Unfortunately the middle class agrees with that, but I don't think that the majority of the French population — and certainly not young people — is living in that world. The city/country opposition shaped the nineteenth century, and the city center/suburb opposition shaped the twentieth century. We are currently living this very latest opposition. On the whole, besides the middle class, we are living in a culture of the city distinct from the suburbs. The city cannot be conceived of without this opposition. It is opposed to its hinterland — which is the case of the nineteenth century — or in symbiosis with it — which is the case of the earlier centuries.

Today, our city culture opposes the center to the periphery, the city center to the suburbs. This opposition is a threat to democracy and to the culture of this end of the century.

In *Open Sky*, you say something that could complete the column that I just quoted: "After the *no man's land* of the desertified countryside, how can we imagine tomorrow the *no man's time* of a planet where the interval of the local space of the continents will have been supplanted by the interface of the global time of the information superhighway?"

The opposition that is developing for the twenty-first century is not the city/country or even the city/suburb one, but the sedentary/nomadic opposition — though not in the sense of Jacques Attali or Félix Guattari.[27] On the one hand, there are those rendered sedentary by a job, who have places of inscription and who are housed, and on the other hand, the nomads who are no longer localized and whose existence drifts from one temp job to another. The twenty-first century will see the return of the sedentary/ nomad opposition on the continent of Europe, which has been made the most sedentary in history.

What you consider post–industrial upheaval is leading us to abandon the city center. What do you mean by a city that no longer has a center?

That means that a new center is emerging. We are witnessing a phenomenon of migration of mid–sized cities toward global cities or megalopolises. The mid–sized cities come together to resist the attraction of big cities like Paris or London. As a result, archipelagos of cities are created to the benefit of city centers which are not necessarily national capitals anymore, but only places of survival in which there is still work available and where one can still subsist by begging. This phenomenon of metropolitanization already existed in the Third World, in which small cities become desertified after the countryside to the benefit of the big cities. This is the globalization of the urban. The center is no longer the center of the city, but cities like Singapore are becoming the center of the world. With respect to a *global city*, city–suburbs are replacing the suburb and the city center. Parallel to this metropolitanization, a hypercenter is being established, a metacity or virtual city that only exists through the urbanization of telecommunications and that is in gestation in the information superhighway. This city is everywhere and nowhere, and each of these world–cities is a neighborhood, a district of this hypercity which resembles the virtual bubble of the economy. It is a virtual city that is produced by the virtual bubble of the economy. So there is an initial movement of metropolitanization in the world-cities and a second movement creating a global hypercenter out of a virtual city that would turn the *global cities* into neighborhoods and all the other cities into abandoned suburbs, like the outlying districts of Paris today.

From the point of view of urban space, what do you criticize in Georges Frèche's position, the mayor of Montpellier, who believes that the department[28] is no longer the measure enabling us to codify urban and regional politics?

Georges Frèche is a historian and he reacts like one. When he says: "If the department was the distance a man could travel on horseback in one day, then today it's the region because one can go farther by car," he is making a completely barbaric comparison. It is an error with respect to the trajectory. A day's journey is a unit of time and place, or even the absence of a unit of place, as with telecommunications. Georges Frèche is still in the transportation revolution. He hasn't realized that we are now in the time unit of telecommunications, telemarketing and telework! His vision may not be departmentalist anymore, but it is still regionalist. So it is not European and even less so global.

In your afterword to *L'Insécurité du territoire* (*The Insecurity of Territory*),[29] it seems that you are frightened by the opening of borders. Aren't you confusing a bit Schengen or the Great Europe with the information superhighway?

I am not worried about the opening of borders: I am not a nationalist. On the other hand, I do worry about the elimination of borders and of the very notion of geographical limits. This amounts to a denial of localization that goes hand in hand with the immeasurable nature of the real time technologies. When a border is eliminated, it reappears somewhere else. When one says: "There are no more borders," this means that the new one has been masked. And I believe that the new borders are defined more in terms of time than of space. Borders, limits and the markings of a field are all related to a use of cadastral or regional space. Yet, now there is a planning of time in addition to the planning of space. We must talk about that limit rather than deny it. The border exists somewhere. When you compare Europe and Africa, the border is actually only aerial or maritime, which is a denial of geography, place and relation. The sea cannot be ploughed, but it has become the last frontier.

A man such as Georges Frèche has forgotten that if the city is the major political form of history, it has a limit. Is a city without limits still a city? My answer is no.

So Los Angeles is not a city?

It is still a city because its opposition is internal, which is to say that its borders are internal. It is a city that extends over 90km. However, it is not size that determines the border, but rather the place where the border is located. In Los Angeles, the borders are inside the city, between the gangs, between the social or ethnic categories...

To no longer take into account the outer border of a city, whatever its size may be, in turn causes that border to be created inside the city.

You also quote the mayor of Philadelphia?

Yes. When the first riots occurred in the sixties, the mayor of Philadelphia said: "The borders of the State are now moving inside the city."

Are you afraid of this movement?

Completely. From the moment that the national border is eliminated, internal borders of identity are created which necessarily lead to war. So, cities and limits go hand in hand, the city is the law, and the law is the border.

What does it mean "to preserve a national space" when we want to achieve a supernational State such as Europe?

The Nation-State is torn between two necessities. At the top, in the European Community, or even the world community, where the national State is surpassed by the possibility of a transnational State, and at the bottom by the will for regional and decentralizing emancipation. This double movement is suicidal for both democracy and politics. When the national State is pulled simultaneously at the top and the bottom, there is no remaining transnational State and there is a movement toward the State of civil war, which is the case of the Eastern countries.

We should have gone from a national State to a transnational State, skipping decentralization, which could only occur in a transnational State. As soon as the State gave power to the regions, it lost its own power on a bigger scale and catastrophe was inevitable. I am in favor of transnationalization or multinationalization in Europe, but I am not in favor of simultaneous movement. If the European transnational State had been inaugurated, then we might have been able to decentralize; but decentralizing at the same time that the European community is being created seems quite irresponsible to me. The same double movement was pursued in the Eastern countries after the fall of the Soviet empire. They fell apart. We are falling apart now, but in a different way. Not as violent for now, although it has not been proven that the feudalization of regions tomorrow will not create conflicts similar to those seen in the Eastern European countries, namely Yugoslavia. So it is the simultaneity of these two opposing movements that seems frightening to me today.

When de Gaulle launched his referendum on regionalization, the French were opposed to it. It was imposed on them, just as it was for Czechoslovakia, where the politicians were the ones who caused the division of the country. The people of Czechoslovakia did not want it.

So you were in favor of keeping the centralization of the country?

Yes, just long enough to surpass the Nation-State. To create Europe, it would have been preferable to take advantage of the French and British decentralizations without following the model of Germany's Länders.

Don't you think that the European choices that have been made concerning the information superhighway are going to complicate the situation?

Yes. Remember that there is always territory and property. The crisis of the new technologies is a crisis of property that is no longer on a city scale but on a world scale. In this way, the information superhighway, the virtual city and the megacity are bringing about a final rupture — the management of real time. The constitution of a city of information, an *omnipolis*, a "city of cities," is going to further complicate the geopolitical future.

"The megacity
is Babel...
and Babel
is civil war!"

The nineteenth and twentieth centuries are still the reign of geopolitics. In the twenty-first century, however, we are already entering the age of chronopolitics, when real time prevails over real space. The real space of the nation is completely disrupted by the simultaneous advent of the urbanization of real time and the creation of a virtual hypercity that will highlight the chaotic nature of our time.

The model for our world that is emerging behind the delirium of information is Babel, and the Internet is already a sign of this. The megacity is Babel... and Babel is civil war!

You are quite pessimistic!

I paint a dark picture because few are willing to do it. My own work goes hand in hand with other reflection on the city. It only exists with respect to a conception of the city, and this conception is largely determined by belief in technical progress. The same idealism that caused the catastrophes and the ravages of the twentieth century is resurfacing today. I am definitely not against progress, but after the ecological and ethical catastrophes that we have seen, not only Auschwitz but also Hiroshima, it would be unforgivable to allow ourselves to be deceived by the kind of utopia which insinuates that technology will ultimately bring about happiness and a greater sense of humanity. Apart from Hannah Arendt, no one has really re-entered this debate. So the work I'm doing is like backfire or resistance. Serge Daney used to say: "In wartime, you don't talk about the resistance."[30] The new technologies, as well as the media in the broadest sense, are like the German

Occupation. My work is that of a "resister" because there are too many "collaborators" who are once again pulling the trick of redemptory progress, emancipation, man liberated from all repression, etc.

Gilles Deleuze was quite fond of the expression "society of control." In your opinion, does the hypertechnologizing of our societies lead to the excessive surveillance and monitoring of individuals?

We cannot understand the development of computer science without its cybernetic dimension. It is not by chance that we're speaking about cyberspace. The information superhighway is related to a phenomenon of feed–back or retroactivity. We are faced with a phenomenon of interactivity that is tendentiously depriving us of our free will so as to bind us to a system of questions/answers that cannot be evaded. When people vaunt the world brain by declaring that humans are no longer human but neurons inside a world brain, and that interactivity favors this phenomenon, it is more than just a question of the society of control — it's the cybernetic society. Taking the model of bees or some other self–regulated system, it's the very opposite of freedom and democracy.

The information superhighway is therefore going to set up an interactive system that is as daunting to society as is the bomb to matter. According to Einstein, interactivity is to the computer bomb what radioactivity is to the atom bomb. It is both a constitutive and dissociative phenomenon. Of course, there is the possibility of numerous and renewed exchanges, but at the same time the threat of control over societies is completely intolerable.

In *Open Sky*, you talk about the "sudden swelling of the present all over the world" and you say: "We can better guess now that the elimination of the political boundaries of Europe and the world is just the tip of the iceberg — the warning sign of a temporal catastrophe where what submerges and disappears is not only the resistance of distances but also that of the dimensions of material space." What do you mean by "temporal catastrophe?"

It's not easy to answer that. I think it's better to write about such difficult subjects than to talk about them. Yet, the being is situated, it is *hic et nunc*. Human beings exist in the three dimensions of chronological time — past, present and future. It is obvious that the liberation of the present — real time or world time — runs the risk of making us lose the past and future in favor of a presentification, which amounts to an amputation of the volume of time. Time is volume; it is not only space–time in the sense of relativity. It is volume and depth of meaning, and the emergence of one world time eliminating the multiplicity of local times is a considerable loss for both geography and history. We are going to witness the accident of accidents, the accident of time. It is no longer the accident of a particular time in history like Auschwitz or Hiroshima. Like time, any trajectory also has three dimensions: past, present and future; departure, voyage and arrival. No one can be deprived of these three dimensions, either with respect to time or trajectory, which means that I go toward the other, that I go to far away places. However, the hyperconcentration of real time reduces all trajectories to nothing: the temporal trajectory becomes a permanent present, and travel — from here to there, from one to another — a mere "being there." Michel Serres calls this the "hors-là" (out there). (Think of the image of the *Horla* in literature: it's a phantom.)[31] We are therefore risking an accident of time that will affect our entire being.

What relationship do you see between time and light?

World time and a single present replacing the past and the future are related to a limit speed which is the speed of light. We have just hit the barrier of real time, which is to say the barrier of light. The destruction of world-space and historical time is possible because we have implemented light and, consequently, its speed. We have achieved a cosmological constant — three hundred thousand kilometers per second — which represents the time of a history without history and a planet without a planet, the time of an Earth reduced to immediacy, instantaneity and ubiquity, a time reduced to the present, which is to say to what happens instantaneously. This is an annihilation and extermination of world-space — a relative, local planet — and of a time — human time — to the benefit of another space and another time. This is not an apocalyptic event but a cataclysmic one on the order of time. At the end of my life, my work on speed has led to the following observation: having reached the acceleration barrier, we have reached a stage that cannot be surpassed. For the first time, history is hitting a cosmological limit — the cosmological constant of three hundred thousand kilometers per second. This is an event which I cannot describe because it is infinitely beyond me.

In his own time, Pascal fought against perspective in painting. He accused it of turning away the interest of the gaze from the divine object. Are you by any chance a defender of the perspective of local space?

I repeat, there is nothing gained without loss. Our society has reached a conclusion: there is no true atheism. After two centuries of industrial and scientific revolution, the annihilation of the god of transcendence and monotheism has put into orbit a god-machine, a *deus ex machina* — the god-machine of information which succeeds the god-machine of atomic energy. We cannot act as if we were non-believers. From now on, you have to choose your belief: either you believe in technoscience, in which case you're a supporter of technical fundamentalism — or you believe in the god of transcendence. Claiming to be an atheist is an illusion. Today, atheists are actually devoted followers of the god-machine. Next to the mystical fundamentalisms and the dramas that they incite, there is the drama of technical fundamentalism related to the *deus ex machina*. As for perspective, that of the *quattrocento*, it is a way to organize the vision of the world. However, our current vision of the world is no longer objective (graphic) but rather teleobjective. We live in the world through a representation that collapses the background and the foreground, as in zoom photographs, and that makes our relation to the world one in which the near and the far are all mixed up. Just as the perspective of real space was the organization of a new optics — geometrical optics with vanishing points and convergent optics —

"The god-machine of information succeeds the god-machine of atomic energy."

the perspective of real time is the implementation of another optics, wave optics. we are no longer confronted with the problems of sun rays and light, we are faced with the problems of electromagnetic radiation. Wave optics conveys signals (digital, video and audio) that organize a relation to the teleobjective world. Everything is collapsed onto a single surface, the interface of the monitor or the visiohelmet.

It is therefore necessary to have a political understanding of wave optics as opposed to geometrical optics. Geometrical optics made the city centers and the suburbs. Centralized cities such as Palmanova are the result of perspective vision. The ideal city of Piero della Francesca is a vision of the city that implements perspective vision. Now, the invention of a perspective of real time and electromagnetic wave optics demands an understanding of what the city of that vision of the world will be — virtual city, hypercenter, etc.

Just as I am against a world time that would eliminate the difference between local times, I would also be completely opposed to a perspective of real time that would eliminate the perspective of real space. This space thanks to which I situate myself with respect to the person next to me, the one that touches me in the physical sense and not in the sense of captors... The problems of the plurality of world visions and the relations to world time emerge as major political problems at this end of the century.

Merleau-Ponty developed a philosophy of perception, Gilles Deleuze developed a logic of perception,[32] and in your latest book you talk about an ethics of perception which, in your opinion, must be taken into

consideration. Aren't you ultimately defending a politics of perception?

In any event, I am opposed to a politics of perception that already prevails with television and the reign of telesurveillance. If I speak in terms of an ethics, it is because the politics is already in place. A colonization of the gaze prompted and forced by the *mise en scène* of information and by the temporality and instantaneity of the montage and framing of events, seems like an important event to me. But the politics of the gaze is television, and this politics will develop with the new captors.

A positive and accidental example of *live* television is the liberation of Nelson Mandela. He was supposed to be freed at three o'clock in the afternoon and every television station in the world was there to witness his release from prison. However, this liberation was delayed. It was out of the question for these stations to give up and go off the air because no one knew when he was going to be released. So television was stuck in chronological time. It was no longer in the time of immediacy, since the time of Mandela's liberation was unknown and uncertainty reigned... And during that half–hour, they stayed there and waited for Mandela's release while watching young girls playing together and zooming on cars that were arriving but that were empty, etc. Television had become if not mute, then at least subjected to waiting. It was no longer in the event just taking place or that had just taken place, but rather in the anticipation of an event. So for once television was outside of this ocular drilling, this drilling of the gaze to immediacy which in some way represents an asphyxiation of the viewer's perception.

According to you, the "tyranny of real time" leads to the disappearance of democracy. How can we resist this?

The tyranny of real time is not very different from classical tyranny, because it tends to destroy the reflection of the citizen in favor of a reflex action. Democracy is based on solidarity, not solitude, and man has to reflect before acting. Now, real time and the world present demand a reflex from the television viewer that is really a kind of manipulation. The tyranny of real time is tantamount to a subjugation of the television viewer. The temporality of democracy is threatened, because the expectation of a judgment tends to be eliminated. Democracy is the expectation of a decision made collectively. *Live* democracy, or automatic democracy, eliminates this reflection and replaces it with a reflex. Ratings replace elections, and the microchip card replaces deliberation. This is extremely dangerous for democracy in terms of the decision and voting time. Ratings and polls become electoral. The poll is the election of tomorrow, virtual democracy for a virtual city.

How can we avoid being devoured?

First by taking back language. Salvation will come from writing and language. If we recreate speech, we will be able to resist. Otherwise we run the risk of losing both speech and writing. Also, by taking back others so as not to lose them, or by refusing divorce. If our societies continue to move toward a solitary individuality, with the divorced couple and the single parent family, no resistance will be possible. So again, by taking back language, talking to each other again and taking back the other, getting back together and not breaking up. Today, we exchange gestures, but fewer and fewer words. Working women and men make gestures, make love... but as for speaking together, it's the "silence of the lambs."

Finally, we have to take back the world. We must no longer fantasize about the beyond the world, the beyond the Earth and the beyond humanity. The beyond the Earth is the conquest of space, "going away to the stars." This is an illusion, because there is only one inhabited planet. Astronomers and physicians don't consider any other planet habitable. It is possible that somewhere in the infinite space of the universe there are thousands of inhabitable planets, but for the time being, there is no other planet but our own. As for creating an artificial atmosphere on Mars or the moon, who are they kidding?

We must also stop fantasizing about the beyond humanity of robotics. A number of books talk about the surpassing of humans by artificial intelligence and medical care technology, as if Frankenstein was coming back. There is nothing beyond humanity. In this respect, humanity is terminal, it is the end of God's miracles, as Hildegarde de Bingen said. It is not the center of the world, it is the end of the world. Humanity cannot be improved. There is no eugenics of the human race. The fantasy of the beyond Earth is its annihilation, and the fantasy of others is their annihilation in favor of the angel–machine.

This angel-machine is in fact a prince of the Apocalypse. You often take the stock market crash of 1987 as

an example of preemptive flight, which foreshadows, in your opinion, the general accident that is threatening us. Is there a way to avoid such catastrophes? By constantly predicting a general accident, aren't you afraid of being labeled a prophet of doom?

Faced with this exacerbation of capitalism, I see no other alternative for the time being but resistance. Yet, it's true that the problem of the accident continues to obsess me. The accident is an inverted miracle, a secular miracle, a revelation. When you invent the ship, you also invent the shipwreck; when you invent the plane, you invent the plane crash; and when you invent electricity, you invent electrocution... Every technology carries its own negativity, which is invented at the same time as technical progress.

And the Internet?

Internet has its own negativity, but the development of technologies can only happen through the analysis and surpassing of these accidents. When the European railroads were introduced, the traffic was poorly regulated and accidents multiplied. The railroad engineers convened in Brussels in 1880 and invented the famous block system. It was a way to effectively regulate traffic so as to avoid the devastating effects of progress, train wrecks. The sinking of the *Titanic* is a similar example. After this tragedy, SOS was developed, a way of calling for help by radio. The explosion of the *Challenger* space shuttle is a considerable event that reveals the original accident of the engine in the same way as the shipwreck of the first ocean liner.

“

The accident
is an inverted
miracle, a
secular miracle,
a revelation.

”

Today, new technologies such as the Internet are a result of the communication revolution. They cause immaterial accidents that are infinitely less observed — with the exception of unemployment, which is a consequence of automation. So work on the accident is critical. Work on science can only advance through work on negativity. However, the dimension of the accident has changed, and we are faced with the emergence of an unprecedented accident. All technical objects brought about accidents that were specific, local and situated in time and space. The *Titanic* leaked in one place, while the train derailed in another. As for us, we have created the possibility of an accident that is no longer particular but general, and this through the interactivity, the networks and the globalization brought about by the communication revolution. So there is an accident brewing that would occur everywhere at the same time. This is in no way a pessimist's hypothesis, but a reality, and the stock market crash is a sign of what's to come. In fact, "interactivity is to society what radioactivity is to matter." Radioactivity is a constituent element of matter that can also destroy it by fission. Interactivity is of the same nature. It can bring about union of society, but it also has the power to dissolve it and disintegrate it on a world scale. We are faced with an original phenomenon: the emergence of the accident of accidents. It is a temporal phenomenon whose only reference is in the philosophy of time.

For Epicurus, time is the accident of accidents. We have reached the speed of light with e-mail, interactivity and telework. We are now creating a similar accident. This is a considerable event that would demand at the very least some criticism, and not merely the advertisement of Bill Gates.

Could you expand upon this notion of the accident that seems so important to you?

For the philosopher, substance is absolute and necessary, whereas the accident is relative and contingent. So the accident is what happens unexpectedly to the substance, the product or the recently invented technical object. It is, for example, the original accident of the *Challenger* space shuttle ten years ago. It is the duty of scientists and technicians to avoid the accident at all costs... In fact, if no substance can exist in the absence of an accident, then no technical object can be developed without in turn generating "its" specific accident: ship = shipwreck, train = train wreck, plane = plane crash, etc.

The accident is thus the hidden face of technical and scientific progress. Every year, for example, the Renault company performs four hundred crash tests at a center designed to improve the safety of its vehicles. However, one thing that must be considered here is the preponderant role of the speed of the accident, thus the limitation of speed and the penalties for "exceeding the speed limit."

With the acceleration following the transportation revolution of the last century, the number of accidents suddenly multiplied and sophisticated procedures had to be invented in order to control air, rail and highway traffic.

With the current world–wide revolution in communication and telematics, acceleration has reached its physical limit, the speed of electromagnetic waves.

So there is the risk not of a local accident in a particular location, but rather of a global accident that would affect if not the entire planet, then at least the majority of people concerned by these teletechnologies.

On this subject, consider the stock market crash of 1987 that resulted from the implementation of the *Program Trading* of automatic stock quotations on Wall Street. It is apparent that this new notion of the accident has nothing to do with the Apocalypse, but rather with the imperious necessity to anticipate in a rational way this kind of catastrophe by which the interactivity of telecommunications would reproduce the devastating effects of a poorly managed radioactivity — think about Chernobyl.

Incidentally, I am planning a museum of the accident with Japan, and a few years ago, I directed a major television program there on this theme.

You talk about "taking back language, taking back the other and taking back the world." In your articles, you seem to be a defender of representative democracy. Can you explain your critical point of view on the new judiciary democracy that began in Italy with the *mani pulite*[33] operation and that continued here in business?

I think the political parties are both threatened and threatening. Judicial revolt, the republic of judges, could only have happened because of the existence of a media class. If you can't understand the role of television inside the civil courts in the United States or Italy, then you can't understand the emergence of the legal class. What is disturbing is not that the judges are doing their job, but rather that they had to climb on the shoulders of the media class in order to get rid of the political class. It is disturbing that they were duped and that they took advantage of the threat represented by the media class to the political class in order to get out of a bad situation. Berlusconi, after Ross Perot, succeeded in breaking the barrier of politics and, for the first time in recent history, the opposition was no longer between the left and the right, but between media and politics. The judges were the agents of this success. The fact that Di Pietro[34] was tempted by political life clearly shows that it was a conspiracy.

With the O.J. Simpson trial, we saw what a *live* trial could be under the eyes of the cameras. The jurors were lynched and, under pressure from the media, they could not make a free verdict.

In reference to Bernard Tapie,[35] the prosecuting attorney stated: "He who is inflated by the image will die by the image." Isn't this commentary a bit too circular?

These are the words of someone who is trying to make a witty statement but doesn't know much about the complexity of the teletechnologies or about the effects of the sorcery of the media.

In your descriptive work on the high technologies, haven't you moved from an ecological conception to an ethical conception over the last twenty years?

Absolutely. However, after the fall of the Berlin wall in 1989, I realized that we were all deterred during the Cold War — actually, someone should write a book called *The Deterred*, just as Dostoevsky wrote *The Possessed*. In everything we have done over forty years, we have been influenced by deterrence. Our way of working, our ideas and our ideals have been influenced by the possible end of the world. And deprived of freedom, we have suddenly found it necessary to get out of this culture of deterrence and anxiety, to free ourselves from it.

History is starting again, and from now on, we can no longer rely on deterrence — whether or not there are nuclear tests will not change the situation. We are therefore living in great distress, and we have lost some degree of assurance. I have a lot of trouble reorienting myself in this age when the threat keeps proliferating. In the past, there was only one threat represented by a harmful object, the atom bomb. Today, however, the threat has become widespread and every single object (objects of communication, transportation, energetics...) must be taken into consideration. My work as "philosopher" and analyst of technology is becoming superhuman. We have lost Jacques Ellul,[36] and recently Deleuze, who was also interested in technology through the desiring machines, so the work is becoming superhuman.

From

likely

war

to

reconquered

landscape

From
likely
war
to
reconquered
landscape

IV

From Likely War To Reconquered Landscape

Leaving the culture of deterrence, leaving the Cold War, doesn't that also mean once again entering the culture of war, as Philippe Delmas[37] suggests?

Completely. The Gulf War and the war In Yugoslavia have shown that from the moment deterrence started to dissipate — it's still there, although deprived of its previous structural form — all wars and civil wars became possible again and then broke out. Conflicts in cities such as Los Angeles and those in the suburbs of France clearly show that the history of war logic is starting again. In this respect, I'm back in my element. However, this threat is so great that the factors are all mixed up. A military Babel has risen out of nuclear proliferation and generalized terrorism; we're disoriented and can no longer find our way, not even in our theoretical work.

Don't you think you were a bit hasty in your analysis of the Gulf War? You suggested that there was a movement from a war of battles to a war of non–battles. Yet, in the former Yugoslavia as well as in many

other countries, another war model exists that is different from the Gulf War model. How do you reconcile these two opposing models in your work?

As they say in France, I am an old intellectual of defense. Like André Glucksmann[38] or Alain Joxe, I work on military problems because I'm a *war baby*. So I don't think I'm being hasty, even if I work on haste and speed! There have always been two kinds of war: civil war on the one hand, the *stasis* of the Greeks, social metastasis, and national or international war on the other. Now the Gulf War was a world war — it was Saddam Hussein against the world — managed in real time by satellites that determined the response of the Patriot missiles to the Scuds.

Yet, the war in Lebanon, the former Yugoslavia, and the war of the Intifada in Israel are a different kind of war. They're all civil wars, internal wars, intestinal wars. They represent the end of civil peace and the disintegration of the social body. They are wars of immediate proximity associated with hatred of the other, and they cannot be compared to Verdun or Stalingrad. That said, the new technologies were used in both cases. The wars in the former Yugoslavia and Lebanon would have been inconceivable without television. They were sparked and fueled by the media of hatred conveyed by free television. So this phenomenon is also related to rapidity and immediacy. After Kusturica[39] read my work, he said "Television kills faster than bullets."

On the one hand, we have a war in real time, one waged from space with satellites and stealth planes; on the other hand, a war in the real time of the media that incites people to crime. And these days, I find it completely legitimate when certain media are sanctioned by the CSA for stating, "It's great to kill a cop." With talk shows, the media is tempted to become the media of hatred by inciting the masses to crime.

To say that there was a civil war in Yugoslavia is clearly to have a political point of view. It can also be argued that these are wars of national liberation.

By "civil war," I mean that there is neither collusion with outside powers nor invasion. The war in the former Yugoslavia was a divorce resulting from a forced marriage.

Coming back to the Gulf War, in what sense do you believe it is the sign of wars to come?

Let me first remind you that the war really happened, contrary to what Jean Baudrillard maintains.[40] The sign of war to come is that the Gulf War was waged from the skies by satellites, that orbiting *deus ex machina* that manages the time of war. It was not only the first miniature world war, but also the first war in real time.

I see two events: the beginning of the war and the end of the war. First, the *cruise missiles* were launched from the battleship *Missouri*, and then the Iraqi soldiers surrendered. *Cruise missiles* are highly sophisticated robots for which the "vision machine" (the title of one of my books) will soon be invented. Equipped with an electronic map, they were supposed to follow a secret path and hit the target by entering through one window instead of another. Such accuracy required both permanent radar plotting to check if the missile was aligned with its electronic map, and an automatic vision machine to pick the window when the missile got in close range, in case the map was inadequate. The launching of these *cruise missiles* marks the beginning of robot war, and the fact of sending out robots against men is clearly an event signaling the electronic warfare of tomorrow: *cyberwar*. However, all this had already been tested in Vietnam with the drones.

What are drones?

Drones are unpiloted planes that scope out enemy territory. They are launched with captors, radar, video, thermography... and keep watch on the battlefield of the enemy.

For the duration of the war in Lebanon, there were *scouts* (this is the name given to the drones sent by Israel) measuring six feet that flew over Beirut to try to track Arafat. They were equipped with videography and thermography enabling them to detect the heat of Arafat's car in order to constantly identify his location. At the end of the Gulf War, forty Iraqi soldiers isolated in the desert saw a drone arrive that was circling around them. They left their trenches and surrendered to the drone. This is the very image of the end of the warrior. Surrendering to a flying camera is a terrifying image. Seeing this drone arrive, the Iraqi soldiers dropped their weapons because they knew that the highly sophisticated artillery of the Americans would blow them up. With the eye flying over them, they had no choice but to surrender to this

"At the end of the Gulf War, forty Iraqi soldiers surrendered to a drone. Surrendering to a flying camera is a terrifying image."

eye. These images illustrate the current progress of drones. The latest drones will be nanotechnological, which is to say that they will be no bigger than a wasp (Ernst Jünger wrote *The Glass Bees*).[41] Work on drones is heading toward the miniaturization of insect–sized microcameras that will be sent to swarm over the enemy. From now on, the eye of God is everywhere. This is telesurveillance — not of the city, but of the battlefield.

Do you think that this excessive technologizing of war, which tends to eliminate soldiers, can explain the fact that we have only been able to send out soldiers of peace... and not of war?

Somalia and the former Yugoslavia showed us that the humanitarian and the military are connected. This is a scandal that the ONG's are well aware of.[42] In a globalized society, world war gives rise to a world police. The armed forces become police forces. From now on, all armies will be the world police. The UN is the forerunner of the world police force. Telesurveillance is one of the elements of the city police. Information satellites and drones will transform the national army into a world police force. On the one hand, there is electronic war — *cyberwar* — the war of information or knowledge; and on the other, there is police intervention to prevent anarchy in the world–city and to keep the chaos of the poor under control. The forces of rapid action already are police forces. In the summer of 1995, the cybernetic war had its first maneuvers in Europe at Camp Hohenfeld. The Pentagon is working on the revolution of military affairs. Alain Joxe and I have therefore decided to work on the computer bomb. Information requires military control. Information is so powerful now that it must be controlled by the military. All work currently done consists in developing this power of information in order to create a veritable weapon of world deterrence. The atom bomb gave rise to the computer bomb. It was useful on two conditions: that there was deterrence and that it never be used. However, it was used in Hiroshima and Nagasaki, as well as in test bombings. During the Cold War, the prevention of nuclear war meant that information structures related to the conquest of space had to be developed. You had to show that you were powerful. A weapon that no one talks about cannot be a deterrent. The computer bomb is a result of both the atom bomb and the need for deterrence. Today, deterrence by the atom bomb is counteracted by the end of block politics. However, the computer bomb and the power of information are assuming considerable proportions. The problem then arises of a deterrence by computer science, wisdom and knowledge. As Goebbels, propaganda leader of the Third Reich, said, "He who knows everything fears nothing." So, the power of information can become an absolute power. Thanks to computer science, it would be take building a power great enough to dissuade those who want to cause destruction in this world–city and question social peace. After nuclear deterrence, it would take societal deterrence by information. If computer science can know everything with its drones and its satellites, then the power of deterrence will be so great that the masses will stop moving. This utopia clearly demonstrates the future of this technological insanity.

Do you really believe that war has been globalized to such an extent? Don't you tend to ignore the wars of national liberation which are often wars of resistance to aggression?

It is true that all forms of war and weapons simultaneously exist today, from knives and stones to the atom bomb. Yet there is a trend toward rationalization. Political war was invented in the city. The mayor of the ancient city was known as the strategist in the Greek city. Before the urban political form was invented, war was chaos, unorganized confrontation. It was the equivalent of barbaric conflicts. Yet once war is rationalized, the political form of war is created — ramparts, the assembly of men in the agora . . .and this by way of rules.

Today, a world society is forming with the tendency to try to regulate violence and war, to give it form. The war in the former Yugoslavia became interesting once it stopped being a civil war. I'm thinking of the Croats who won a normal victory, which is to say a victory of troops who fought other troops in the field. At that point, the war changed in nature because it was formalized. The victory of reconquest by the Croatian troops restored to the war the form it had lost, thus allowing the great powers to intervene; for as long as the war remained a battle of all against all, nothing could be done.

A new form of war is looming on a world scale that might be the beginning of the first real world war — because let me remind you that WWII was not truly a world war, no more than WWI. With the new technologies, the possibility to regulate or formalize a world war and to counter it with defense becomes a probability. This is a trend. Perhaps it will all come crashing down and degenerate into chaos, and then we can witness a global Yugoslavia. The United States is threatened by civil war and disintegration. So are France and Europe. Just look at England or the suburbs in France. So all this might result in a global civil war, in chaos, in a *stasis* of the Nation-States before economic problems and mass unemployment as well as the impossibility to control social problems.

In your recent work, you talk about the new weapons; would you say that the military officers you work with are aware of the imminent dangers?

Yes, particularly after the Gulf War and the Yugoslavian conflict. The role of the communication weapons was recognized by many soldiers. During the Gulf War, the French arsenal lacked night vision machines, AWACA planes used to monitor the battlefield, satellites other than Spot, etc. Today, the French are aware that communication and information weapons are decisive compared to weapons of destruction, and so there has been an attempt to militarize information. An information staff has been created, and all signs indicate that an information war will soon replace traditional war.

The purchase of the AWACS after the Gulf War, the putting into orbit of the Helios satellite to compensate for the limitations of Spot, the more systematic use of drones by France... All this proves that virtual war is on the march and that the French military is right in questioning the stakes of such a war. Yet, during this war, the French weapons systems were so far behind those of the United States that France could not fully assess these reversals.

You are vehemently opposed to electronic money, and you are worried about the appearance of financial bubbles. You have also spoken frequently about the stock market crash. What does an urbanist such as yourself have to say about money?

The return to bartering in the suburbs and in the cities of England is certainly not a good sign. It represents an economy of survival — you do what you can with what you have — but I won't be tricked by the overcoming of money and the return to a barter system. This is the sign of a serious regression, which is one of the effects of the virtualization of economic power. Wealth and speed have always been connected, one being the hidden side of the other. Moreover, the use of plastic money is a good example of this movement that has made circulation synonymous with money. Money is nothing, circulation is everything. Money was not originally what it is today. People paid with grains of salt, shells or little pieces of bronze, in other words with objects that were concrete, material, and most of all countable. Consequently, an initial dematerialization is underway with the promissory note and the check — the countable is losing its dimensions. Salt has three dimensions, whereas the promissory note only has two. With electronic money, this dimension disappears, replaced by an electromagnetic impulse.

And so equivalence disappears at the same time?

Yes, and the speed of circulation has supplanted money. The production that resulted from this three–dimensional money is itself eliminated in favor of pure speculation, in other words a pure electronic game. The movement of dematerialization which I analyzed in reference to the city and the neighbor reappears in the case of money. The logic is exactly the same, in other words the aesthetics of disappearance, and what is disappearing now is production and its monetary referent. We exceeded the limit of the speed of exchange with the *Trading* program that combined the stock markets into one. Wall Street, London, Frankfurt and Tokyo are now just one stock market. I have no choice but to oppose this move toward the absolute limit.

What is your conception of money beyond this critique of plastic money?

I'm a territory man, not an economist. Territory is not a milieu, but speed–wealth and automatic quotations are. A milieu is capable of supplanting a territory, and this is a phenomenon that I cannot accept. I'm a property man — which is not to say that I'm a landowner. I am in favor of things with depth. However, the depth of property is being eliminated by the superficiality of computerized exchange.

What type of space would you be inclined to defend in the name of property?

I'm a voyager. Being Italian on my father's side, I don't consider myself a nationalist. I'm French by language, though I don't feel attached to any country. I'm an Italian *beur*,[43] and therefore an exile. However, I am nostalgic about inscription in a depth of space and time, a depth of relation to the other, and a depth of meaning. Gilles Deleuze worked a lot on this, which must explain my interest in his work.

Property is only one step away from the house...

I think that architecture is the first real measure of the Earth. Its function is not merely to house or shelter man from the elements — the cave was good enough for that. The dimensions we live in must then give meaning to the scale of both the neighborhood and the world. The dimensions that we assume in a house are the beginning of a relation to the world, and the quality of a landscape is related to the architectural quality of our habitat. I talk about gray ecology, because we will have to consider this question of dimensions on a world scale, although we have already considered it on a city scale. Living in a neighborhood is not the same as living in an apartment. The dwelling is the indicator of dimensions, as well as the indicator of my relation to the world. Architecture is a measure of the world.

We hear more and more about preserving landscape. Landscaped parks are being built where the old Citroën buildings are; and in Limousin, they're trying to save the Millevaches plateau... What do you think of a politics of landscape?

It goes without saying that it represents the work of recovery from a great disaster, this being the fact that European territory was left to lie fallow. In *The Identity of France,*[44] Fernand Braudel said that the immigrant problem was never really a problem — all of Europe is merely a history of migration — but that conversely, a Europe without peasants is unheard of. European space was a veritable garden. Its great desertification and its being left fallow are a drama that must be corrected like all the others. Today, however, correcting means masking. The appeal of landscape is nostalgia for the extraordinary garden of the *sweet France* of the peasants. Landscape is what lies beyond environment, yet at the same time it's a bandage on a wooden leg. There are three terms that are closely related: milieu, soil and territory. Soil is the most fundamental inscription in a rural or an urban space. Territory is already a liberation of the soil by modes of transportation or communication. Milieu is physical and yet abstract. Today, the interest in landscape will have to go through the discovery of the event landscape.[45] Human presence must be reintroduced, otherwise we will all have been collaborators in the desertion of the countryside.

What is an event landscape?

If we consider the rural landscape, there are more landscapes than events. If we consider the urban landscape, there are more events than landscapes. A lot more things happen among men in the city than in Beauce, even if the cultures, the seasons, etc., constitute events. Today, it is essential that the question of the event landscape be addressed — and not the question of *land art* underlying today's museographic debates. How can we account for what happens in something that moves very little or not at all? How can we conceive of space as a stage for men and not merely a somewhat nostalgic object of contemplation? A dramaturgy of landscape has to be reinvented. A scenography of landscape has to be restored with actors and not merely spectators. The rural landscape that was lost when left fallow was an event landscape of the civilization of men by way of the vine, wheat, etc. The history of the countryside is a factual history even more important than the history of the city, but it has been forgotten.

Concern for landscape is not new. In the eighteenth century, Girardin[46] was already developing a philosophy of landscape or tamed nature.

True, but the word landscape comes from painting or depiction on canvas. It's essentially the achievement of an aesthetics of landscape. "Landscape is a state of mind," said Amiel.[47] More than a simple problem organizing perspective, this is what happens in that landscape. In other words, it's the investment of a population that lives this landscape just as Péguy[48] lived his relation to Chartres. I'm neither a pantheist nor a naturalist; I am in favor of an event landscape.

Where does the expression "event landscape" come from?

It comes from a theological vision. For God, history is an event landscape. Battles and big events are the same as great forests and tall trees. It is an image of the action landscape that takes place somewhere and that must be recovered. Otherwise we will not have resolved the situation in the suburbs.

In your opinion, why are the suburbs falling apart?

Because they're not a landscape. There is no investment. If there is a state of mind, it's monstrous, it's hell. The suburbs have all the comforts one could want, but there is no state of mind, except for the infernal nature of this abandoned place.

Could you give me an example of a landscape that is particularly livable?

Everyone has an inner landscape. Some prefer the sea, others prefer the mountains, the countryside or the desert. Everybody has a mental landscape that organizes their relation to the world. Everybody has their own inner painting. My inner paintings are the coast and the desert. I am a littoralist and not a sailor. I need a horizon that is wide and changing. The coasts of Brittany are my favorite landscape, with their cliffs and the clash between the liquid and the solid. I also admire the changing atmospheric nature of the wind and the light. So it's a relative landscape — the interface between earth, sea and sky. It's a place where relativity is acted out through both static and dynamic forces.

And the desert?

It's like the sea. It evokes the feeling of our presence on a planet. I like landscapes where you can feel the planet, where the territorial body of planet Earth is tangible on a smaller scale. I love the local when it enables you to see the global, and I love the global when you can see it from the local. We must keep these both together and never lose them.

Théodore Monod said that he would have liked to die in the desert. As a philosopher of space, don't you think that there is more for a man than being able to choose his landscape of life and death?

I knew Théodore Monod.[49] We even fasted together for peace in Taverny in front of the nuclear command post. He is a man with "depth" who also reminded me of Abbé Pierre. Yet, the body proper can only exist in a world proper. There can be no body proper "in and of itself."

Personally, I was born in Paris but wouldn't want to be buried there. I'd rather be buried in Normandy, not far from the landing beaches where I walked around for a very long time. And if I had to choose the landscape of my death, it would be a small cemetery near Douvres-la-Délivrande in Calvados, halfway between the coast and the plains.

NOTES

1 Vladimir Jankélevitch, French existentialist philosopher. He wrote books on Bergson (*Henri Bergson*, Paris: Presses Universitaires de France, 1959), Schelling (1933) and Hegel. He was equally interested in music: *De la musique au silence* (1974–79).

Jean Wahl, French philosopher. He wrote extensively on existentialism: *Philosophies of Existence: An Introduction to the Basic Thought of Kierkegaard, Heidegger, Jaspers, Marcel, Sartre* (London: Routledge and Kegan Paul, 1969); *A Short History of Existentialism* (Westport, CT: Greenwood Publishing Group, Inc., 1972).

Raymond Aron (1905–1983), French sociologist, historian, political commentator. He was known for his skepticism of ideological orthodoxies. A highly influential columnist for *Le Figaro* and *L'Express.*, Aron enjoyed a position of intellectual authority among French moderates and conservatives, rivaling Sartre's hold on the left. His rationalist humanism was often contrasted with the Marxist existentialism of Sartre. One of his most influential texts was *The Opium of the Intellectuals* (New York: Norton, 1962), in which he criticized left-wing conformism and the totalitarian tendencies of the left.

2 L'Abbé Pierre is a popular French priest known for his active support of the poor. He has also been attacked, more recently, fo rhis support of a Holocaust revisionist historian. The Priest Movement was an attempt by the Church, after WWII, to reclaim the working class by sending priests to work in the factories.

3 Paul Virilio, *Bunker Archaeology* (New York: Princeton Architectural Press, 1994).

4 Alain Joxe is a French political author and academic who writes on problems of military logistics and terrorism.

5 Georges Perec was a sociologist and experimental writer active in the OULIPO (Potential Literature) movement. He is the author of numerous fictions, including *Life: A User's Manual* (Boston: David R. Godine, 1987).

6 *Esprit* is a progressive Christian magazine, *Causes Communes* a leftist magazine, and *Traverses* the magazine of the Centre Pompidou which Virilio edited with Jean Baudrillard in the 1980s.

7 Félix Guattari, activist, anti-psychiatrist and philosopher, is the author of *Chaosophy* (1995) and *Soft Subversions* (1996) (New York: Semiotext(e), Foreign Agents Series. He wrote *Anti-Oedipus* (New York: Viking, 1977), and *A Thousand Plateaus* (Minneapolis: University of Minnesota Press, 1987), with Gilles Deleuze.

8 Radio Free France was the organ of the Gaulist "France Libre" government in London during WWII.

9 Henri de Saint-Simon (1760–1825), French theorist and one of the chief founders of Christian socialism. F. Engels recognized that his writings contain *in embryo* most of the ideas of the later socialists. After

1928, the influential Saint-Simonian movement advocated social and economic planning by scientists and industrial leaders as a way of "improving the conditions of the poorest class."

10 Paul Virilio, *The Vision Machine* (Bloomington: Indiana University Press, 1994).

11 "Objectif" in French also means "camera lens," and "téléobjectif" means telephoto or zoom lens. [Tr.'s note].

12 Maurice Merleau-Ponty (1908–1961) was a leading proponent of Husserl's phenomenology in France, which grounded philosophy in bodily behavior and perception. His major works are *Phenomenology of Perception* (London: Routledge and Kegan Paul, 1962) and *The Structure of Behavior* (Boston: Beacon Press, 1963).

13 Roland Barthes, *Camera Lucida: Reflections on Photography.* Translated by Richard Howard. (New York: Hill and Wang, 1981).

14 Yves Lacoste is a well-known French geographer and historian. He wrote *Dictionnaire de géopolitique*(New York: French and European Publications, 1993) and *Ibn Khaldun: The Birth of History and the Past of the Third World* (New York: W. W. Norton and Co., 1985).

15 "Hiroshima Mon Amour" was directed by Alain Resnais from a script by Marguerite Duras.

16 Gilbert Simondon's most influential work is *Du Mode d'existence des objets techniques* (Paris: Aubier, 1958); also, *L'Individu et sa genèse physico-biologique* (Paris: Presses Universitaires de France, 1964).

17 Norbert Wiener (1894–1964), a prolific mathematician, coined the term "cybernetics." Alan Mathison

Turing (1912–1954) was an English mathematician primarily noted for his work in mathematical logic and machine computation. He was widely considered to have set the terms of reference for the field of artificial intelligence. Claude Shannon is the author of *The Mathematical Theory of Communication,* which provided the basis for information theory. His work has had a great impact on the field on communications engineering.

18 Paul Virilio, *Open Sky* (London: Verso, 1997).

19 See Sylvère Lotringer and Paul Virilio, *Pure War* (New York: Semiotext(e), 1983, 1997).

20 In 1990, Félix Houphouët-Boigny, president of the Ivory Coast, spent $150 million building Our Lady of Peace Cathedral, the biggest in the world, in the town of his birth, Yamoussoukro. He offered it to Pope John Paul II as a gift, which was accepted. There was some criticism about spending so much money in a time of economic hardship. The cathedral, meant to be a grandiose imitation of St. Peter's Cathedral in Rome, has a capacity of 18,000 worshippers, and the surrounding square accommodates 30,000 more.

21 Patrick Poivre D'Arvor, French television personality and "news anchor," hosts a literary television program. He has garnered a bad reputation for a fake interview he claimed to have conducted with Fidel Castro.

22 Khaled Kelkral was a young Algerian involved in the bombing campaign of the early 1990s that brought Islamic fundamentalist terrorism to France. He was shot dead in September 1995 by the French police in a village outside of Lyons while he was being filmed by a television crew.

23 Timisoara (in western Romania) is the site of the December 1989 Romanian uprising, which lasted ten days, during which the communist dictator, Nicolae Ceausescu, was overthrown. The new provisional government at the time falsified evidence, claiming a death toll of about 5,000, including 800 children. If any, it was less than 100 dead.

24 Marvin Minsky, an expert in the field of artificial intelligence and a pioneer of media arts, is currently the Toshiba Professor of Media Arts and Sciences at MIT. He is also the Director of the MIT Artificial Intelligence Laboratory, a co-founder of the MIT Artificial Intelligence Project, a sometime advisor to NASA and an employee of Disney. He wrote *Computation: Finite and Infinite Machines* (Englewood Cliffs, NJ: Prentice Hall, 1967); *Computers and Artificial Intelligence: A Science Masters Series Book* (New York: Basic Books, 1989) and *The Science of Mind* (New York: Simon and Schuster, 1988). His recent work, on CD-ROM, demonstrates how artificial intelligence can serve as a model for the human mind and consciousness.

25 Paul Virilio, *Speed and Politics* (1986) and *Popular Defense and Ecological Struggles* (1990) (New York: Semiotext(e) Foreign Agents Series).

26 Minitel is the successful French Internet service provided by France Telecom to both business and residences. The Minitel terminal is a clunky box distributed by France Telecom for accessing Minitel services. FT boasts that there are currently 6.5 million terminals in use in France, as well as 600,000 computers using software which emulates the function of the box.

27 Jacques Attali, a one-time advisor to French president François Mitterand, has written many books on both music and politics: *A Man of Influence* (Chevy Chase: Adlerand Adler, 1987); *Millennium: Winners and Losers in the Coming Order* (New York: Random House, 1992). After the advent of faxes and cellular phones, he announced the birth of a high-tech, privileged nomadism quite at a variance with Guattari's nomad machine. Cf. *Nomadology* (New York: Semiotext(e), 1991), with Gilles Deleuze. Also *Chaosophy* (1995) and *Soft Subversions* (1996), *op. cit.*

28 A French "département" is an administrative division which is smaller than a French region. Recently France has been divided into twenty regions (and not just into departments).

29 Paul Virilio, *L'Insécurité du territoire* (1976) was recently republished by Éditions Galilée, 1993, with an important afterword by the author.

30 Serge Daney is a French film critic and cult figure who died a few years ago. He wrote for *Cahiers du Cinéma* and the leftist paper *Libération.* His most important book is *Ciné Journal, 1988–1986* (Paris: Cahiers du Cinéma: Diffusion, Seuil, 1986. Foreword by Gilles Deleuze).

31 See Guy de Maupassant, *Le Horla* (Paris: A. Michel, 1984).

32 Gilles Deleuze, *Francis Bacon, Logique de la sensation* (Paris: Éditions de la différence, 1981).

33 Operation "mani pulite" was the name of a team of anti-corruption prosecutors from Milan led by Antonio Di Pietro. At one point, almost one thousand people were arrested in a bribery and kickback scan-

dal, including a former Socialist prime minister, Bettino Craxi, and a fifth of Italy's parliament. In 1994, Di Pietro left the legal profession to pursue a political career. In 1997, he won a landslide victory in a senate by-election.

34 Sylvio Berlusconi is the head of Fininvest, the media group which controls three Italian television networks and 65% of Italian TV advertising. Elected on a wave of popularity based on his anti-corruption stance, he became prime minister of Italy in 1994. However, after less than ten months in office, he was accused of having authorized bribes to tax officials as part of the "mani pulite" investigations, and was forced to resign.

35 Bernard Tapié is a flamboyant French entrepreneur/politician/tycoon who managed to "rise from the ashes of his reputation." He headed the French center-left party. In 1990, he purchased 80% of the struggling Adidas empire. In 1992 he was chosen to be the new Minister of Urban Affairs. One year later, he was involved in a bribery scandal involving his Olympic de Marseilles soccer team, and charged with defrauding the Credit Lyonnais. In 1995, Tapié was declared bankrupt and was ordered to pay back $245 million in loans.

36 Jacques Ellul, a philosopher, theologian, and sociologist who died in 1994, analyzed the way technology shapes thought and action. His major book is *The Technological Bluff,* translated by Geoffrey W. Bromiley (Grand Rapids, MI: W. B. Eerdmans, 1990).

37 Philippe Delmas, a military analyst at the French Department of Foreign Affairs, is the author of *The*

Rosy Future of War (New York: Free Press, 1997). The fragility and instability of countries whose status began eroding during the Cold War, he alleged, will be the main cause of wars to come.

3 André Glucksmann is one of the "nouveaux philosophes" who direclty linked Marxism with Stalinism in the 1970s. His major books are *Le Discours de la guerre* (Paris: L'Herne, 1967), *Strategie et revolution en France* (Paris: Éditions Bourgois, 1968), *Cynicism and Passion* (Stanford: Anma Libri, 1976), and *Les Maitres penseurs* [*The Master Thinkers*] (Paris: Éditions Grasset, 1977),

39 Emil Kusturica is a Yugoslav film director. His films include "Do You Remember Dolly Bell" (1981), "When Father Was Away on Business" (1985), "Time of the Gypsies" (1989), "Arizona Dreams" (1993), and "Underground: Once There Was a Country" (1997).

40 Jean Baudrillard, *The Gulf War Did Not Take Place* (Bloomington: Indiana University Press, 1995).

41 Ernst Junger, *The Glass Bees* (New York: Noonday Press, 1961).

42 O.N.G. stands for "Organisme Non Gouvernemental d'intérêt public ou humanitaire," or Non–governmental organization for public or humanitarian concerns [Tr.'s note].

43 "Beur" is a term currently used in France to designate children of North African immigrants born on French soil.

44 Fernard Braudel, a leader of the prestigious group of French historians, L'Ecole des Annales, published a number of books, including *The Identity of France*

(London: Collins, 1988) and *Civilization and Capitalism, 15th–18th Century* (New York: Harper and Row, 1986).

45 Paul Virilio, *Paysage d'Evénements* (Paris: Galilée, 1996).

46 Émile de Girardin (1806–1881) was a French journalist and novelist. Born in Paris, in 1836 he started *La Presse,* which was the beginning of journalism for the masses in France. At first on the side of the regime of Louis Philippe, he moved towards the left and finally became a Republican.

47 The Swiss writer Henri-Frédéric Amiel (1821–1881) was born in Geneva, where he later became a professor philosophy at the University of Geneva. He is mostly known for his *Journal Intime,* which he kept fully from 1847 until his death. Published in English in 1885, it clearly reveals the silent tragedy of a man paralyzed by his supersensitive cerebral existence.

48 Charles Péguy (1873–1914) was a French nationalist, publisher ad neo-Catholic poet. Deeply patriotic, he combined sincere Catholicism with socialism, and his writings reflect his intense desire for justice and truth. His important works include *Le Mystére de la charité de Jeanne d'Arc* (1910), *L'Argent* (1912), and *La Tapisserie de Notre Dame* (1913). He was killed in World War I.

49 Theodore Mondo, naturalist and scientist of the desert, is the author of *Bonjour le Sahara du Niger: Air, Tenere, Djado* (Lyon: Créations du Pelican, 1994). Monod believes that deserts stir peoples' emotions because they represent nature as it was before the arrival of human beings.

BIBLIOGRAPHY

Breton, Philippe. *Une Histoire de l'Informatique.* Paris: La Découverte, 1987.

_____. *L'Utopie de la Communication: le Mythe du Village Planétaire.* Paris: La Découverte, 1995.

Guisnel, Jean. *Guerres dans le Cyberspace: Services Secrets et Internet.* Paris: La Découverte, 1995.

Jaffelin, Jacques. *Pour une Théorie de l'Information Générale.* Paris: ESF, 1993.

Laïdi, Zaki. *A World Without Meaning: The Crisis of Meaning in International Politics.* Translated by June Burnham and Jerry Coulon. New York: Routledge, 1998.

Negroponte, Nicholas. *L'Homme Numérique.* Paris: Laffont, 1995.

Popper, Karl. *Un Univers de Propensions.* Combas: L'Éclat, 1992.

_____. *La Télévision: Un Danger pour la Démocratie.* Paris: Anatolia, 1994.

Rachline, François. *Que l'Argent Soit.* Paris: Calmann-Lévy, 1993.

Rheingold, Howard. *Virtual Reality*. New York: Simon & Schuster, 1991.

Rosnay, Joël de. *L'Homme Symbiotique: Regards sur le Troisième Millénaire*. Paris: Seuil, 1995.

Roszak, Theodor. *The Cult of Information*. New York: Pantheon Books, 1986.

Serres, Michel. *Les Messages à Distance*. Paris: Fides, 1995.

Toffler, Alvin and Heidi. *War and Anti-war: Survival at the Dawn of the 21st Century*. Boston: Little, Brown, 1993.

Virilio, Paul. *The Art of the Motor.* Translated by Julie Rose. Minneapolis: U. of Minnesota Press, 1995.

_____. *Open Sky*. Translated by Julie Rose. New York: Verso, 1997.

Von Neumann, John. *The Computer and the Brain*. New Haven: Yale University Press, 1986.

Weisenbaum, Joseph. *Puissance de l'Ordinateur et Raison de l'Homme*. Paris: Informatique, 1981.

Wiener, Norbert. *Cybernetics and Society*. New York: Executive Techniques, 1951.

Woodrow, Alain. *Les Médias: Quatrième Pouvoir ou Cinquième Colonne?* Paris: Le Félin, 1996.

INDEX